LEARNING AT HOME

Alex Griffiths and Doroth
London-based movement
Teachers) to involve paren
The movement has spread
has counterparts in similar
of the country. The idea is
everywhere, and has bee
educational and national press.

Alex Griffiths and Dorothy Hamilton have also written a handbook for teachers: *Parent, Teacher, Child: Working Together in Children's Learning* (Methuen, 1984).

ALEX GRIFFITHS · DOROTHY HAMILTON

Learning at Home

The Parent, Teacher, Child Alliance

Illustrated by Pat Dymond

CEDAR

A Mandarin Paperback
LEARNING AT HOME

First published in Great Britain 1987
by Methuen Children's Books Ltd
This edition published 1992
Reprinted 1992
by Cedar
an imprint of Mandarin Paperbacks
Michelin House, 81 Fulham Road, London SW3 6RB

Mandarin is an imprint of the Octopus Publishing Group,
a division of Reed International Books Limited

A CIP catalogue record for this title
is available from the British Library
ISBN 0 7493 1047 2

Printed and bound in Great Britain
by Cox & Wyman Ltd, Reading, Berks

CONTENTS

ACKNOWLEDGEMENTS

We should like to thank Alec Williams for the use of his extensive knowledge as a children's librarian, and Jennifer Dey, Margaret Matthews and Roger Pearce for their comments, as parents, on our final drafts. Our gratitude also to Margaret Bradshaw of Durham University and to Ruth Merttens of the Polytechnic of North London, for their professional advice. And a special thank you to Kate, Paul, Sarah and Rebecca and to Deryck, for their support and patience during the preparation of this book.

INTRODUCTION

This book is intended to help you help your children with their learning, in co-operation with teachers. Its theme is that children learn best when the adults around them work together to provide them with good learning opportunities.

Not so long ago, we would have said that writing a book like this would probably be a waste of time. No-one really expected parents and teachers to co-operate so closely over children's education. But attitudes have changed to such an extent that both teachers and parents now want to work *with* each other: the days of teachers saying 'leave it all to us' have thankfully almost disappeared.

As the evidence in Chapter 1 will show you, it is now well established that when parents and teachers work together in a partnership, they bring about a great improvement in children's learning. This book, a companion to our book for teachers, draws on our own experience to answer some of the questions most often raised when people are trying to build up a good parent-teacher-child partnership. In Chapter 2, for example, we look at the central question of how you and your child's teacher can keep in touch with each other, and ask how each of you – your child, yourself, and the teacher – benefits from this kind of co-operation.

Working together is not always easy, and in Chapter 3 we look at the main principles underlying the way children learn, and the best ways we know to help that learning forward. Where teachers and parents can agree on good educational practice, this provides them with common meeting points. And in Chapters 4 to 9 we see how these principles can be applied in the fields of reading, writing and mathematics – putting extra emphasis on reading, as it is so vital both in itself and as the basis of most other subjects.

The school curriculum, even as expressed through the National Curriculum, cannot really be so neatly separated out as our chapter headings suggest – all learning is interrelated, and we only split it into 'subjects' for convenience. So throughout the book we try to give examples of learning that run across these subject divisions, showing for instance how mathematics is dependent on language development.

We have not attempted to include everything there is to say about children's learning, as a different book would need to be written for each child to cater for individuality! Instead, by outlining what we believe to be the principles of good teaching, and giving plenty of practical ideas, we have tried to help you and the teacher to find the best way forward for your own child. Many of the ideas you will find familiar, and will be putting into practice already. We know this, but if we didn't include some of the more obvious points we would be failing to give a picture of good practice as a whole.

Of course there will be difficulties, and we have tried to cover these as they are likely to occur – e.g. reading difficulties in Chapter 6 – as well as reserving Chapter 11 for more general difficulties. We included a special chapter for secondary age children as they can be helped differently, also because their schools are larger and more complex than primary schools, and often seem less approachable.

To avoid repeating ourselves, we should like to make it clear at the beginning how we define a 'parent'. A parent is a mother, father or step-parent – but in some circumstances could be a grandparent, friend, houseparent, social worker, older sister or brother, or whoever is in a position to help. Nor do we expect any of these to be a 'super-parent': no one person can do everything. Don't feel guilty about what you can't do, concentrate on what you can do.

Again and again we shall emphasise that you and your child should *enjoy* learning. Without enjoyment, very little will be learned, and little progress made. We hope you will enjoy this book, and that you can use it to contribute to your child's learning in partnership with teachers.

ONE

Can Parents Really Help?

There is no doubt that the days when parents were obliged to leave education to the school are on the way out, and parent-teacher co-operation is on the way in. Nowadays, educationists believe it is essential that parents should be involved in their children's schooling, and that without such involvement, children are disadvantaged. Parents guide their children in learning to talk, as well as to walk, feed and dress themselves, and a multitude of other skills, so why shouldn't they be well equipped to help educate their own children later?

Unfortunately, many parents have been discouraged from helping with such important skills as learning to read, and it is with these very skills, researchers have shown, that parents can do most to help. Where parents and teachers are prepared to pool their knowledge and expertise, children gain greatly. This may seem like common-sense, but common-sense has not always prevailed! Now the traditional divide between home and school is breaking down, and parents, instead of being asked by teachers to leave the teaching to them, are being gradually brought in from the cold.

Since the sixties, schools have been encouraged to involve parents in general school life, and since the seventies in the early stages of their children's learning. In 1975 a major government report on reading[1] placed an emphasis on parents reading to their children to help with 'reading readiness', just in the very early days of schooling. But nowadays most of us accept that parents can do much more. So why the change in attitude?

The change has come about because of the results of recent research involving parents. One outstanding example is provided by the work of a research team in Haringey.[2] For two years, top infant and lower junior children were regularly heard reading by their parents, from books sent home by the class teacher. These children improved significantly more in their reading than those who did not receive parent help, and it was also found that they did better than children given extra reading help at school.

The PACT (Parents, Teachers and Children) project in the Inner London Education Authority has gone further by demonstrating that children of all ages can be helped by their parents.[3] In one class of eleven year-olds, the motivation to read was so strong that the school had to divert almost the whole of its money allowance one year to buying new and more wide-ranging books!

Other education authorities have carried out and investigated projects of their own. For example, eight inner-city primary schools in Coventry took part in a scheme to involve parents in reading and other language skills.[4] After two years' work, it was found that these children had very positive attitudes toward reading, that their free writing and spoken language was of a very high quality, and that their actual reading skills were far better than had been thought possible. Such results are remarkable – they should convince any teacher, parent or educationist of the value of parental involvement.

We have quoted research concerned mainly with reading, as this is still the major area of investigation, but other projects have shown that parents can help in virtually any area. PACT schools are already involving parents in mathematics and other subjects with great success.

As schools set out to involve parents more in their children's learning, there is a good chance you will be approached and asked to help. Some schools will invite you into the classroom and ask you to help with the work going on there; but this book is concerned with the help you can offer your child at home, while keeping in touch with the teacher about what you are both doing.

There are two main ways in which you can help with your children's learning at home. One is by making time to sit down and work together in the evening, perhaps using books and other materials sent home by the school. The other is through the kind of learning that can take place at any time, and might be called 'incidental' learning. As we have said, educators split learning up into subjects – but learning is a whole, and children are continually learning from their everyday experiences. They learn especially through their own play. The distinction we make between 'work' and 'play' does not mean much to children, for whom, as often as not, play is work. By the same token, the closer we can make work to playing, the more likely our children are to learn. As parents, you are well placed to help with this kind of learning – by joining in with your children's play, encouraging them to share your occupations, and pointing out new things to learn as they arise. We try to give you plenty of ideas for both kinds of learning in the course of the book.

Parents can work very successfully with their children without any assistance from teachers, so if co-operation from your child's school is not forthcoming, go it alone – it's not as difficult as you might believe, as we hope this book will show. But working in isolation can never be as effective as a co-operative effort, and wherever possible you should try to work with your child's teachers. We think you will find that most teachers will be prepared to work with you to devise an individual, tailor-made approach for your child. If they're not, try showing them this book!

The help you can give your children never really ends. Even fluent readers and good mathematicians still have much to learn. Your aim should be more than the acquisition of the basic skills: your real aim is to encourage in your child a love of learning. This applies to everyone – all children can benefit from their parents' help, including the so-called 'slow learners' and 'dyslexics', and any parent can help, even if they cannot read well or speak English. We cannot claim it is always going to be easy, but if you are prepared to give up a little time on several days each week, then over the years your child will reap the benefits of your help. Remember your children's learning is rooted in their early experiences at home, and they need you to provide a steady continuation of those experiences.

Your children are yours, and you have the right to help them in any way you can. But rights also carry responsibilities. Taking these seriously puts the onus on you to find out the best ways to help: our next chapter suggests how you can best work with the teacher.

TWO

Working with the Teacher

We start this chapter optimistically, by assuming that your child's school is interested in working with you, and has already approached you for help with your child's learning. We know many of you will not be so lucky: if your own child's school has not yet fully accepted the value of parents as partners, you will need to approach it tactfully, and we discuss ways of doing so later in the chapter. Meanwhile, though, what might you expect from a school that is actually asking for your help?

A likely starting-point

The most common area in which schools work with parents is that of reading. There are many reasons why reading is chosen, the main one being that everyone – not only teachers and parents, but children too – recognises how important it is, both as an essential skill in its own right, and as the basis for most other learning. This makes it a common meeting-point in education. Also, it's very enjoyable – the teacher can feel that sending home a good book is something that parent and child can share with pleasure, not like the old-fashioned idea of boring homework. Teachers may well feel that a child stands a good chance of getting a better experience of reading at home than in a busy, noisy classroom.

Probably you will get an invitation to the school, to discuss the way you and the teacher can work together. The schools who are most successful at involving parents don't just send home a book and hope – they take time to explain their point of view and listen to yours, and they make regular opportunities to talk over how things are going. They will probably have a way of communicating with you besides these meetings – for instance, many use a 'record card', which your child carries to and from home with the current book. This card has space on it for parent and teacher to jot down notes for each other, and it forms a useful record of the child's work.

Such a card has many possible uses. You can say what you think of a book or piece of work your child has brought home, tell the teacher if you're pleased with or anxious about your child's progress, make suggestions, and ask questions about anything you want to know. All this in addition to your remarks about the actual work your child did that evening. On the other hand, there's no need to write much, or even at all – some people prefer just to tick the card, or record the number of pages read. Nor need it always be about work – we have known whole conversations going to and fro about lost socks! The important point is that you and the teacher keep in touch regularly.

No-one would suggest that the record card is any substitute for talking to one another in person; it can't provide enough space to do more than keep up the contact till you actually meet again. But the combination of regular meetings and the record card puts parents and teachers in a very good position to share their information and experience.

Let's look at what each side of the new partnership has to offer and how it can help your child.

What you gain

Your child's teacher has had a long training in education, plus experience of children's learning in the classroom. This adds up to a useful body of knowledge, and there is no reason why you shouldn't share some of it. Teachers can not only give you advice about the best ways to help your child, but can explain why those ways are likely to be the best. Many of you are already helping your children with reading, writing and mathematics – but parents often worry as to whether they are working in a way the school would approve. Parents also ask: if we are working differently from the school, won't this confuse the child? (how many of us have cringed at the cry: 'We don't do it that way in school!'?) There's no need to make too much of a point of perfect consistency, since children are quite tough creatures, and survive all sorts of different approaches. Teachers often teach quite differently from each other anyway – and indeed there is an argument to be made that children get a richer educational experience from working with different adults, who each have their own approach to learning. Even so, there is no doubt either about the value of co-operation and agreement on essentials – so go to the school and find out how they *do* do it!

More broadly, you can get to know about the whole background to your child's life in school – what he or she is doing during the school day, and why. This picture of their child's 'other life' is something parents are entitled to, yet a surprising number never manage to find out. Try to meet all the teachers who are involved with your child from time to time, perhaps for specialist subjects. It's not at all unreasonable for you to want to get a feel of the whole school and what it is trying to do.

What the teacher gains

However much you may learn from the school, never forget that you have unique knowledge about your child, and don't be afraid to share it. You have an understanding of your child that only a parent can have. Parents have shared their children's early lives, nursed them when they were ill, taken them on holidays, visited relatives – and generally known them in thousands of situations that the teacher never sees. Moreover, parents have taught their children many basic skills in the early years of life, and will have insights into their own child's way of learning that will help the teacher to teach the child. Education is nowadays so much based on the individual child's interests, that teachers really do need the information parents can supply about a child's life experiences, likes and dislikes, fears and interests.

Teachers gain also from the fact that they now have help with their teaching load, not only with specific tasks like reading, but with broader learning through home situations. If you and the teacher talk about your child's play and interests, you can plan together ways of encouraging 'incidental' learning which can involve all kinds of areas of the school curriculum. We haven't space to go into all the possibilities of this kind of learning, which deserves a book to itself, but we try to hint at it as we go along, and you will find one or two examples in the last chapter.

The different knowledge and understanding that parents and teachers each possess is complementary; between you, you will be far better equipped to work out the best ways of teaching your child than either of you would be alone.

What your child gains

It will be obvious from what we have just said that we think your child will quite simply be better taught if you are working with the teacher. But children also gain emotionally and socially. After all, parents and teachers are the most important adults in a child's world. To have that world split in two as it has been in the past is, if you stop to think about it, a strange and uncomfortable state of affairs for a child to have to cope with. When parents and teachers really talk to each other, children show us time and again how much this means to them.

Their world makes more sense: when they do something to be pleased about, everyone else knows and can be pleased too. And where things go wrong, how much better if this gets talked about as part of ordinary day-to-day communication, and not as a special nasty event.

This last point is important if your child is going through a difficult patch at school. Without a big extra fuss, you and the teachers can work out what is happening and why, and how best to tackle it. Schools have always informed parents about children's 'bad' behaviour, and asked for 'co-operation' in handling it; but often the most this would amount to would be an interview between parents and the head teacher – from which the parents might come away feeling like naughty children themselves. Many schools now realise that involving parents more seriously than this may be the most effective way to help a child through a difficult period. Sometimes a written record is kept by both parent and teacher about what is going

on in home and school, so that it can be talked over in detail, and definite problem areas pinpointed. Or a parent may sometimes be asked to come into the classroom for a time, to help support a child who is having difficulties of one sort or another. Children respond far better to this sort of concerted effort than where adults are working in isolation. The result may well be a happier, and so less difficult, child.

Last, but certainly not least, parent-teacher co-operation really does make a difference to children's actual learning, and their wish to learn – and this is our main reason for writing this book. It's a very effective message to children to show them that the most important adults in their lives are hand-in-glove over the learning business.

Older children

Much of what we've said in this chapter so far has been based on primary schools. If you have a child in secondary school, you may be feeling that all this talk about 'your child's teacher' is all very well – but you are faced with a bewildering number of teachers, and perhaps little chance to talk to any of them. We grant it's not so easy at secondary age – nevertheless, the principle behind everything we have said so far still applies. No one by now should be in any doubt that we think children of all ages need their parents and teachers to work together, and that applies just as much to young people in secondary schools.

It's quite a new idea for parents to be involved at all with junior and secondary learning, apart from the odd bit of help with difficult homework. So you and the teachers are likely to be breaking new ground as you decide how you can be involved in your child's learning. Obviously, parents who have worked with teachers right from their child's first schooldays are going to be at an advantage in finding ways of helping later – but it will be some time before most parents are in this position. Fortunately, there are already ideas being worked out in secondary schools that have involved parents very successfully (see Chapter 10).

The unco-operative teacher

And now, what about teachers who haven't yet realised the value of working with parents? If your child's school is like this, is it possible for you to do something about waking it up? Parents don't usually like the idea of 'pushing' what they think at a school, fearing that this will affect the teacher's attitude toward their child. Anyway, they argue, surely the school must know best? The fact is of course that schools and teachers make mistakes just like anyone else, and they do need the occasional push. Schools have often been nudged towards new attitudes by concerned parents. In East London, we ran a stall in a street market to explain to parents what PACT was about. Hundreds of parents stopped to talk – and quite a number went away to ring up their child's school and ask why parents weren't helping there, as they were in the school just down the road. Such consumer pressure galvanised several schools into enquiring about the idea, though they hadn't seemed especially interested before!

So while it's always a good thing to be tactful, remember that you have the arguments on your side. Be aware too that teachers may be more apprehensive about meeting you than you are of meeting them. While parents have tended in the past to feel diffident about challenging the 'expert' authority-figure of the teacher, teachers themselves often feel unsure in their dealings with parents. Incredibly, the subject of meeting and co-operating with parents in any serious way has simply never been covered in most teacher training. So bear all this in mind when you are approaching an apparently unco-operative school – it may be that you are the first to break down the traditional barrier in this case, and perhaps you will be more welcome than you expect. It may help too to find other parents who feel the same way as you do about helping with children's learning – there is always strength in numbers. We're *not* advocating bullying tactics – just persuasion!

Occasionally, you may meet a teacher who will use 'jargon' to discourage you. This kind of in-language is perhaps supposed to suggest that only teachers are competent to help children learn. Bear in mind the plain truth that in the end no one really knows exactly what causes a child to learn. The best we can do is to point to situations in which learning is most likely to happen, and here parent-teacher co-operation has produced the best research results of the lot. So just press politely forward in the face of 'expert' resistance, and don't let the professionals put you off. If they really are professional, they will want the children to learn, and that is what will matter most to both of you.

If, in spite of all your efforts, you aren't getting anywhere with your child's teacher, ask for an appointment with the head teacher, or with one of the school governors, to put forward your point of view. Your parent governor should be able to help you to get the ear of the school management. You could try donating a copy of this book to the school to support your arguments! In the last resort, if the only way to make your point is to antagonise the teachers, which you know is going to be unhelpful for your child in the long run, then you may have to consider a change of school. But this is a last-ditch strategy – a better way by far is to keep trying for co-operation, and to bear in mind that even a little co-operation can go a long way.

A cautionary tale

We'll end this chapter with a warning: a story about a teacher and parents who hadn't thought it necessary to keep in touch with each other about the progress of six year-old Carl. His teacher was very pleased with the good progress he was making with his reading. Following the tradition of the school, she sent him home with his reading book every night to read to his parents, thinking that this was all that was necessary in the way of co-operation between home and school. Carl read most days to his teacher. His style of reading was slow and stumbling, with frequent pauses to 'sound out' words. One day Carl's mother tentatively asked the teacher why Carl was reading the books he brought from school so slowly, in contrast to the way he read his other books at home. It turned out that Carl had learned to read long ago at home, and could cope easily with reading matter that some ten year-olds would find difficult. He had been mimicking his friends' reading style, because he thought that was the 'proper' way to read in school! 'I felt so awful' said his poor teacher. 'If only I'd known earlier I wouldn't have wasted so much of Carl's time!'

Summary

1. Keep closely in touch with your child's teacher. Take advantage of any schemes by which the school offers to co-operate with you over your child's learning.
2. Learn from the teacher, find out about the school and its methods.
3. Make sure the teacher learns from you!
4. Co-operate over your child's emotional and social development, as well as learning.
5. Don't be put off by the extra difficulties of contacting secondary school teachers.
6. Approach unco-operative schools and teachers with tact but firmness. You have the arguments on your side.
7. Don't leave it to chance – talk to the teacher regularly. This does matter for your child's future.

THREE

Good Teaching: Some Basic Principles

Once you and the teacher have decided to work together, you will want to know that you have firm common ground to work from. Above all, this will mean argreement about the best ways to encourage children to learn. You will find there are basic principles for good teaching that most teachers and educationists recognise. They are not difficult to remember, since for the most part they're based on sound common sense; and you will need to bear them in mind when you are helping your child. We have summarised them under seven brief headings:

1. Enjoyment and relaxation.
2. Interest and purpose.
3. Praise.
4. Never too long at a time.

5. Talking and listening.
6. Learning by doing.
7. Using your opportunities.

We'll look at each of these in turn.

1. Enjoyment and relaxation

The first and most important rule is to try to provide a warm and enjoyable atmosphere, with as few distractions as possible. We know this isn't always easy, but your chances of success at home are definitely better than those of a classroom teacher. Although most classrooms are happy enough places, teachers cannot give their undivided attention to any one child for much more than a few minutes at a time – often there can be 30 or more other children competing. And it's the close adult attention that is the most enjoyable thing from the child's point of view.

Try to see that your child feels relaxed, and free from pressure: it is only at home that children can be given constant opportunities to learn at their own speed. This sense of relaxation is something you will want to feel too, of course, so don't work with your child when you think you should be getting on with some nagging job, or when a favourite television programme is on. And if you find yourself getting impatient or irritable, just stop. It isn't worth pushing yourselves if you aren't enjoying it, because in these circumstances it's most unlikely that any worthwhile learning will be taking place. For once, ignore the proverb 'Never put off till tomorrow what you can do today'!

2. Interest and purpose

Interest is closely linked with the last point, since if your child isn't interested in what he or she is doing, it's not likely to be very enjoyable. We hope you will find that the modern materials that teachers send home – especially the books – really are fun and interesting. And this means interesting for you too, which is just as well, since your interest in the work you are doing is very important. Your attitudes are the ones your children are most likely to adopt for themselves, and whether you are aware of it or not, you are providing a model for your child as far as learning is concerned – if it is fun and interesting for you, then it must be a good thing.

We said earlier that education nowadays is based to a great extent on the interests of the individual child; this is quite simply because we know that an interested child is a child who is learning. You have only to look at the prowling toddler, into everything, and learning at probably the fastest rate of his or her life, to see the truth of this. Children's natural curiosity is the most powerful ally the teacher has.

Purpose is closely tied in with interest, of course. Toddlers aren't just curious, they're after very definite purposes of their own. Children are quite exceptionally purposeful creatures – they want and need to master the world around them, and this gives them a very powerful motivation to learn what that world is about. Don't waste this motivation by demanding that your child does work he or she doesn't see the sense of: harness the energy in ways that serve the child's purposes.

3. Praise

Praise your child often – for anything that is worthy of praise (and if you are on the lookout, you will find a surprising number of things that are). Don't just praise for obvious success, but for trying. All children need encouragement to boost their confidence and help them to take the next step forward. Just as with adults, nothing succeeds like success, and this is especially true if our efforts get noticed by someone whose opinion we value. Nor does this apply only to big things like learning to do something new: how many of us feel like doing a routine job, such as cooking or cutting the grass, when we know that nobody's going to notice what we've done? A word of appreciation makes all the difference.

While we don't want to advocate over-praising to the point of absurdity, we must stress that this point about praise is probably the most important one of all. For some reason, it is something that adults too often forget, even though they know how useful it is. Research tells teachers that they don't praise enough – but that when they do remember, it can make the difference between successful learning and no learning at all. So if you don't tell your child when he or she is doing well, even if it's only in very small ways, you run the risk that your work together will be much less productive.

4. Never too long at a time

When you sit down for a learning session with your child, work only for short periods at a time. You will find that ten to twenty minutes may be needed for reading activities, but five might be enough for learning a couple of spellings or doing an arithmetic problem, especially with young children. A few minutes of good learning experience is worth hours of boring struggle, which only puts children off learning. And you have to consider your own time – you are less likely to want to work regularly with your child if the demands you are making on yourself are too heavy.

Remember that while ten or fifteen minutes may not seem long to you, it may be very different for your child. The time you spend working together at home is quite concentrated compared with work in school, and it might be hard for a teacher to give that much individual attention – say, to a child reading aloud – in several days. So your work together may be harder for your child than you realise at first. Overall, bear in mind the maxim 'little and often'.

5. Talking and listening

Talk about the book you are reading or the work you are doing together. And through asking questions, encourage your child to talk, and listen attentively to what he or she is saying. Talking, and listening to each other, is at the heart of language development – and the grasp of language is the high road to learning to think. 'Learning to think' may sound a little strange, but it doesn't happen just by accident in a child. Children brought up having very little to do with adults (as in some of the old-fashioned orphanages) were often handicapped in their ability to think, and found it hard to realise their potential as adults. Thinking, talking, and close, friendly relationships go hand-in-hand in a child's development. Your conversations with your child are at least as important as the actual work you do together.

6. Learning by doing

Especially when they are young, children need to do things in an active way to help them to learn. Sometimes we find this out the hard way – the child who hasn't taken enough notice of your warnings about bumble bees may have to get stung before learning that particular lesson! We all know that there's no teacher like experience. Whatever you are trying to teach your child, see if there is some activity that would help to make the information 'real'. Instead of just talking about metric measurements, measure the furniture, or better still the child; if you find a particularly good story, act it out together; help the child to make a model that demonstrates the principle of the lever.

7. Using your opportunities

This is a general point about the adult's ability to be on the lookout for ways to make the session interesting: to help your child learn from a mistake perhaps, or to relate what you are reading about to the child's own personal experience. Much of the most effective learning is incidental, or apparently incidental, to what is actually being studied. A child learning about, say, volcanoes is much more likely to remember if together you:

a: talk about your own experience of hot, smoky things – the day she burned her fingers on the gas stove?

b: relate the idea to a family holiday – that funny shaped hill;

c: find things to look at together – the lump of pumice that Auntie Jane keeps by the bath; or visit a geological museum;

d: make a model: use sand or earth to make a mound, scoop out the centre and fill it with screwed-up paper, and see how realistic it looks when you set light to it! Older children, of course, can make much more sophisticated models.

If your child's school is running a scheme for involving parents, we expect the teachers to have given you advice along the above lines. Between them, these 'rules' take in most of the fundamental principles underlying good educational practice, and teachers tend to agree that whatever you do, you should be safe if you use them as guidelines. Don't dismiss them just because they sound like common-sense – that is just what they should sound like, but as everyone knows, common-sense is not always followed. Teachers and parents alike need to remind themselves of what they already know.

So keep the points in this chapter in mind when you work with your child. All the research suggests that parents are very good natural teachers anyway, and what we've said should make certain of it in your case!

Summary

1. Talk with the teacher about good teaching.
2. Make sure the sessions with your child are relaxed, and that you both enjoy them.
3. See that your child is interested in what you are doing – it helps if you are, too.
4. Harness children's natural sense of purpose; there's so much they *want* to know.
5. Don't be afraid to praise – most of us can take a lot more praise than we ever get, and it does us good.
6. Keep the learning sessions short.
7. Talk to each other – and don't forget to listen.
8. *Do* things together.

9. **Use any opportunity to make the time more interesting and fun for both of you.**

FOUR

Learning to Read

Having looked at the principles, now for the practice. In this chapter we get down to the practical aspects of working with your child; and we start at what most people think of as the natural place, which is learning to read. An ideal way to help with your child's reading is via the sort of scheme we outlined in Chapter 2, in which schools send home books and a 'record card'. If you aren't lucky enough to have a school that operates such a scheme, we hope you'll try to persuade them to do so, as we've suggested. But failing that, just work at home with your child anyway, and try to talk to the teachers when you can.

Reading is all around us, and children should be encouraged to read the print they meet in their everyday lives – notices, street signs, chocolate wrappers, bus destinations, television programmes – all of which make ideal reading material, because they have meaning for the child. The purpose of being able to check when the football is on the telly is self-evident. This kind of everyday reading – which later becomes much more complex, as when following detailed instructions to get somewhere, or understanding the blurb explaining museum exhibits – is as valuable in helping children with their reading as sitting down with a book. It is also the kind of reading that you as a parent, sharing the 'real life' of your child, are in a better position to encourage than the teacher in school.

We can't however, when we're talking about reading in the next few chapters, always refer to 'books and other reading materials', or to 'stories and information reading', so please bear in mind that when we say 'book' or 'story' we mean all kinds of reading material, and all kinds of subject matter.

When you are helping your child with reading, you will want to know what teachers believe is good practice. To understand this, you need first to ask the important question:

WHY DO WE READ?

The answer is, of course, that people read both for pleasure and for information. And when we teach reading, it is pleasure and information that teachers are hoping to help children discover. That may sound too obvious to be worth saying, but in fact to aim so directly for enjoyment and purpose has completely changed our approach to the teaching of reading. Educators haven't always made such a straightforward link between the 'why' and the 'how' of learning to read.

The traditional way

Quite likely you remember from your own early schooldays a series of books that told you about a boy and girl (Janet and John? Dick and Dora?) who did rather boring things and talked to each other in an odd way. 'See the boats, John. Come, Janet. See the little dog run.' We all know that children don't talk like this, but these books were produced at a time when 'learning to read' was seen as separate from 'real' reading, and so wasn't much concerned with being interesting, or even making sense. For the sake of repeating a few simple words over and over again, books like these sacrificed interest, enjoyment and commonsense. They also sacrificed ordinary, sensible language that children could recognise and understand. As a result, they ended up with dull stories and silly language – a perfect recipe for boredom. They must have helped to put a great many children right off books and reading altogether.

We have to admit that not every school has yet left all those boring 'readers' behind – change like this happens slowly – but you are not likely to find anything quite as bad as the one we just quoted. If you do, help to give it a gentle push toward the school dustbin.

There was, of course, a reason for making the books so repetitive. Teachers thought that what mattered was that children got all the words exactly right, so the same words were repeated over and over again for children to learn by heart. Much more emphasis was put on correctness than on the meaning of the story. Yet, of course, the only reason people read is to get the meaning – we don't read for the pleasure of getting difficult words right! If they don't feel interested in what the reading is about, children simply don't want to learn – where's the reward?For that matter,the old method didn't even succeed in the limited aim it was trying to achieve. For example, which would your football-minded child be more likely to get right in these sentences:

> See the boats, Janet
>
> He kicked the ball into the goal

– 'boats', which he's seen forty boring times, or 'goal', which is a new word to him in print, but which makes sense from his own experience?

The new way

Today we teach children to read for understanding, and that means helping them to find interesting books that they will want to understand. If children don't get all the words quite right, it doesn't matter – the main thing is, have they got the gist of what the writer is trying to tell them ? Understanding what a book is about is a process that can start very early in life, in fact the earlier the better. The first stages of reading go back to the earliest years of childhood, even back to babyhood. Children in their first year of life enjoy 'talking' about pictures and having simple stories read to them. As they start handling books for themselves, they begin to develop 'book sense' – learning to hold the book the right way up, to start at the front and look at the left-hand page before the right, and so on. Gradually they learn the stories, usually by getting you to read the same old favourites over and over again; and before long, they're telling you the story, sometimes even turning the pages at the right places! Encourage this 'learning by heart' – it's an important step on the road to learning to read.

As children follow your finger pointing to the words, they begin to discover the connection between the story and the print. Soon they are picking out familiar words for themselves, and it may not be so long before they can decipher a simple book with just a few words on each page. You will find that this may happen without your realising the difference between this stage and the earlier one. From 'knowing by heart', your child is suddenly reading words out of context, and able to read a page he or she hasn't seen before. This is what teachers call 'learning to read by reading'. It's a lot more natural, and fun, than the painstaking efforts adults used to put into 'teaching' children to read; unfortunately a lot of this 'teaching' probably got in the way of the natural process. What a disaster it would be if we all set out on a formal teaching programme to 'teach' one year-olds to talk!

Reading together

What are the best ways to encourage your child to learn to read by reading? The first rule is to let the child choose books that are interesting and fun to read. Then, to the 'rules for teaching' we listed in Chapter 3, we should add 'frequency' when it comes to the early stages of reading. If you can read together a little every day, so much the better. Try to make a habit of sitting down and relaxing with a book for a few minutes in the evening. But don't see this just as a reading exercise for your child: you could be the one to read sometimes, or you could take turns to read.

The younger the child, the more it will be you who reads, the child joining in where possible – perhaps finding words he or she knows like 'Christmas', or telling you 'what the picture says'. The older the child, the more you will be the listener: asking questions, comparing notes as to what you both think of the book, and whether the writer was successful in getting across what he or she was trying to say. But older children enjoy having a story read to them too, and they often miss out on this because they're considered 'too old'. Think of 'Book at Bedtime' on the radio – why should anyone be too old to be read to? An older child might also appreciate having items from the newspaper read out, or something that interests you both from an information book.

'Taking turns' is an excellent way of reading a book together. You might read a page each, or just change over when the person reading feels like stopping, or read aloud together. At other times, you could read silently together. We shouldn't always insist on getting children to read aloud to someone else, since the main thing we're trying to encourage is the enjoyment of books for the child's own sake. So let children read silently to themselves as soon as they are able, as well as reading to you.

Making mistakes

As your child begins to pick up the rudiments of reading, you will want to know what to do if he or she makes a mistake. Here it's definitely best if you can get guidance from your child's teacher. Children can learn an enormous amount from making mistakes – each mistake is potentially a chance to learn something new – but they do need help at each point, and different schools have different ways of dealing with this. Still, there are general rules which you can use. If a word is causing a problem:

a: It's often best just to say the word yourself, so that your child doesn't lose the story line, and the interest. So simply give the word after a few seconds;

b: If you think your child could get the word with a bit of help, try to encourage a 'good guess'. We put a lot of stress nowadays on the importance of guessing, and it deserves a heading to itself.

Learning to guess

'Guessing' is just a simple word for the idea of bringing the child's own thoughts and ideas to reading. We want the child to 'get to grips' with the mind of the person who is writing, and what that person is trying to say. This is a very important part of reading. We adults couldn't read as fast as we do if we weren't half-expecting what is coming next, getting the sense as we go along. In just the same way, we want to encourage children to make a sensible guess at what is coming next. But, of course, we don't want them to guess wildly, choosing words that the writer couldn't possibly have meant. When a child reads 'I fed the helicopter at the zoo', he or she may be pulling your leg, but certainly not making a sensible guess. Whereas reading 'hippopotamus' would be, even if the word turns out to be 'heffalump'!

There are plenty of clues to help children guess what an unknown word might be. Is there a picture that gives a hint? What is the first letter of the word itself, and the word's shape and size? – clearly, on these grounds it wasn't an emu that was being fed at the zoo. Most of all, what is the sentence *likely* to be about, given what has gone before? – helicopters don't eat, in the usual way. A variation on this 'guessing from the meaning' is to read on to the end of the sentence to see if that will help. You just skip over the difficult word, read 'The m . . . did a good trick – he pulled a rabbit out of a hat' – and the sense of the sentence, together with the first sound 'm', should be enough to help your child to guess the word 'magician'.

Letter sounds and names

Notice we said 'sound'. It doesn't help with reading to teach children the names of the letters, because they don't usually come into the actual sound of the word. Nor do we teach sounds by themselves much nowadays, because that isn't really what reading is about: trying to 'sound out' words can actually prevent a child from getting a word, when a good guess would have been more useful. With a language like English, fifty per cent or more of the time 'sounding out' doesn't work anyway. You lose valuable guessing time, forget the thread of the story, and still get left with 'rog' or 'rowg' when the word you want is 'rough'!

That said though, it's certainly very useful to be able to spot a sound – 'b', let's say – at the beginning of a word to give you a clue. If your child doesn't easily connect up the first sound with the way a word begins, try playing the old 'I-Spy' game, only using the sounds of the letters instead of their alphabet names: children soon pick up the idea when they hear 'bat, ball, Ben, bed, bandage, book, banana' in quick succession.

The one time, by the way, when it is useful to teach letter names is in learning the good old alphabet. This will never go out of fashion while we have dictionaries and reference books, and you will give your child a very useful skill if he or she can recite the alphabet correctly.

Talking to each other

If you find your child is losing the fun of reading because of worrying about getting every word exactly right, try reading a 'book without words' (one that tells a story by pictures alone) together, to encourage the idea that a good story is not just a lot of words. Another advantage of this kind of book is that when you tell the story to each other, you and your child will be using your own language, and this links spoken and 'book language' together in the child's mind, so that the two don't seem too different.

Because written language is not quite the same as spoken language, it takes time for children to become familiar with the different language of books. Once they do, a good book will take children on to discover new ways of expressing themselves.

When you read with your child, you are helping him or her to develop language – and also the ability to reason, and the ability to sympathise with others through characters in the book. This will be especially true if you sometimes talk about the story, wonder what will happen next, discuss what you would have done if you were a character in the book, and so on. Help your child to evaluate the book: see if you agree or disagree that it was a good (or bad) story, whether an information book succeeded in getting its message across, and so on. And where you can, relate the reading to your child's own experience, as we suggested at the end of Chapter 3. Talking, and listening to each other, is at the heart of language and reading development.

Finally, don't forget that you should both be talking to the teacher too – discuss with your child what you should put in the record card.

Mother-tongue reading

If English isn't your first language, you may feel it will be harder to help your child with reading. But there is no reason why this should be so. If you can't read English (in which case we hope a friend will be passing this information on to you), read in your home language instead. All the value of reading will be there in exactly the same way, and the same is true of talking in your mother-tongue. Your child will learn to reason and understand – but with the additional advantage of having two languages to think in. Children benefit from such enrichment of their language.

Don't let anyone tell you the use of two languages confuses children. A child who is forced to stop using one language and start an unknown one, at a stage when language is still developing, may miss out on some of the early stages of learning to think. It's much better to let the two languages overlap naturally. Children seem to find no serious difficulty in this, unless the adults around them imagine it will be difficult, in which case perhaps they make it so!

If you understand spoken English well enough to follow your child reading aloud from books sent home from school, listen and ask what has gone wrong if it isn't making sense. And you could use some of the children's books now published with texts in both English and another language. Finally, if your child is still at the early stages of reading, take the opportunity to improve your own ability to read English at the same time! Children love being the teacher.

What to avoid

If children learn best through enjoyment, then pushing them to do what they don't want to do, or can't do, is clearly counter-productive. Unfortunately adults – parents and teachers alike – are sometimes tempted to hurry a child along. This kind of pressure is rarely useful, and we need to resist the temptation. Children hear such comments as:

> 'For goodness sake, you knew that word yesterday'
> 'Come on, only three more pages and you've finished the book, then you can get onto a higher one'
> 'You shouldn't be reading this, it's too easy for you!'

It doesn't help them, and it may turn them against reading altogether if the pressure gets too much. Children usually know their own pace, and the amount they can comfortably read at a time. We all like to do something easily at times, and adults often choose undemanding books for relaxation, so why shouldn't children? Besides, easy reading gives children confidence and makes it certain that the book is thoroughly understood, which is the most important thing of all.

So don't pressurise – and don't, whatever you do, turn reading into a competition:

> 'Shouldn't you be on a higher book by now? – I'm sure Peter's mum told me he was on Yellow Books'.

If reading is reduced to a race between children, then it has sunk really low. We can't expect children to enjoy books for their own sake if adults have this attitude. The child who is made to feel inferior to other children because of reading may well get to hate books, and no wonder.

No doubt you'll recognise that what we're talking about in all this is the effects of 'nagging'. We all do it, and we all know it doesn't work. If it's a question of muddy boots or untidy bedrooms, it doesn't matter too much. We can allow ourselves the luxury of a good nag now and then just to relieve our own feelings, and know we aren't doing much harm. But if it's a question of our children's attitude to reading, it does matter, very much – and it will go on mattering in the future. This is something that mustn't be damaged by our own feelings of annoyance or impatience. Take the pressure off reading and keep it a pleasure, and that includes leaving it altogether for a time if your child 'goes off' it. Don't worry, the chances are he or she will be back to reading soon enough if you go on showing your own interest, and if the right book or other reading material is found.

All the above, of course, applies to other learning as well as reading. We put it in this chapter deliberately though, because reading is so fundamental to all learning and thinking, and because your child's attitude to it is, therefore, very important. Also, it's in this area more than most that parents are inclined to worry and 'nag'. Remember – nagging is counter-productive. Better that your child ignores books altogether than learns early to dislike them.

Enjoying yourselves

Now we are back to the first principles of learning – interest and enjoyment. It's here that it is most helpful to teachers to have parents reading with their children. Getting fun out of a book, talking about the pictures and the story and so on, is one of the main contributions you can make to your children's learning. You will be helping them to realise that learning can be fun – something they want to do, not just have to do. Teachers know this, and they know that your relationship with your children is your big advantage. You matter more than anyone else does – if mum and dad like reading, then it's obviously a good thing.

Don't worry if you wouldn't turn to a book as an exciting way of spending your own leisure time! Many a parent who hasn't opened a book for years (because it was so boring at school?) has found that the books children are given to read by good schools nowadays, really are worth reading. Bright pictures, good story lines, useful information – all making you want to turn the page and find out what happens next. Such books have sometimes turned parents into readers again. By the same token, don't put up with boring books: send them back and say how it felt to try to read them. From this your child will learn that reading is not just about taking in what someone else has to say, it's also about making your own personal judgement as to whether what is being said is actually worth reading. Reading is about thinking for yourself.

In the next chapter, we deal with aspects of reading development that we haven't covered here. Reading is a huge topic though, and could do with a book to itself. If you need to know more than we have space for in this book, you will find books on reading listed in the bibliography at the back.

Summary

1. Keep in mind the question: Why do we read? Help your child to read for the pleasure of it, and to get the information he/she wants.
2. Don't worry about getting every word right – read for the sense of the story.
3. Help children to 'learn to read by reading'; let them choose books they enjoy, and the rest will probably follow.
4. Talk about the reading and the pictures. Ask questions, and share what you think, too.
5. Read regularly, but not for too long at a time.

6. Take turns reading, vary what you do together. Read to your child, even if he or she is older now.
7. Mistakes: either give the word, or help your child to guess from the sense of the story. Don't try to 'sound words out', though first sounds at the beginning of words are useful.
8. Don't nag, and don't let reading become competitive.
9. Have fun!

FIVE

More about Reading: Good Readers and Problem Readers

At this point you may be feeling that what we have talked about so far is not particularly right for your child. Perhaps you feel that your child is beyond the stage when your help is needed or wanted, or has some difficulty that needs more help than you are able to offer. In this chapter we will consider these questions in greater detail.

The good reader

If all is going well, children will have started to be readers by the time they have left the infant classes, and you can now help with the further development of your child's literacy. Children must learn how to make use of their newly acquired reading skills. So how can you help?

One obvious course of action is to encourage children to read a wider range of materials. Newspapers and magazines, reference books and encyclopedias, poetry and plays, DIY instruction manuals and cookery recipes come to mind as materials which demand more of children. It is quite easy to find opportunities to use some of these, such as when you are working on the car or discussing a topic neither of you knows much about. In this way, the idea can gradually develop that we read for different purposes – for pleasure, for information, to follow instructions and to understand new ideas.

Meanwhile, this wide variety of reading materials will be helping to develop your child's range and use of language. It is not only vocabulary that is extended. Children come into contact with different sentence patterns and structures, and this extends their ability to use language for thinking and communicating with others.

You can help your child to a deeper understanding of the written text by discussing it together. For example, the discussion of a story could centre around such questions as:

'What happened when . . .'
'What would have happened if . . .'
'What would you have done . . .'

Don't forget to put in some of your own answers – it isn't an interrogation, it's a sharing of ideas. While sharing books in this way you can help your children to explore ideas and experiences they cannot have in real life, learn to understand emotions such as hate and love, greed and generosity, and find different ways of behaving towards others.

An activity which will help you put together many aspects of reading is to choose a topic that interests both of you, and work on it together. This search for knowledge and understanding could take you to the library and museums, and lead you into very interesting conversations. One example is provided by Alan, a small boy with a passion for anything electric. It started the day his teacher showed him how to make a simple electric circuit while he was in an infant class. After that, he and his parents found books in the local library, watched television programmes on electricity, made all kinds of electrical gadgets, visited a generating station, and generally became 'experts' in a small way. Alan's parents learned as much as he did, and kept an exhibition of their gadgets in the garage for their friends and neighbours to see. Alan himself ended up in secondary school doing all the lighting for the school show!

Other practical suggestions to try:

- Encourage the use of a good dictionary, perhaps one that gives derivations.
- Introduce your child to the public library, its subject and author indexes, and classification numbers (ask the librarians if you are at all unsure yourself, they are usually very helpful).
- Make sure your child can use the content pages and indexes of a book.
- Don't discourage the reading of easy books or old favourites, children enjoy them.
- Discuss the stories your children have read, perhaps comparing the merits of various authors.
- Try reading the occasional children's book yourself to discuss. You will probably enjoy it – perhaps to the point of addiction!
- Make sure you are seen reading!
- Look at the ideas on reading skills in chapter 10.
- Ask the teacher for further ideas to help your own child.

Perhaps the crucial point to remember is to try and share interest, the rest will follow.

Reading difficulties

Research has shown that one of the most effective ways in which teachers can help with reading difficulties is by involving parents, so just by using the approaches so far outlined in this book, you are probably already helping your child in the best possible way, especially if you are working in close cooperation with the teachers. We ourselves have found that so few children fail when parents and teachers work together along these lines that we almost feel it is unnecessary to add anything further. However, just in case your child is still not succeeding, there are various ideas you can consider.

Before starting on any particular course of action though, it is usually worthwhile checking your child's hearing and vision. Even mild and medically unimportant conditions can delay a child's learning. For example, a number of children have an extremely small hearing loss which for most purposes does not matter – but if they continually suffer from coughs, colds or flu, such losses can become more noticeable and slow down learning. Hearing and vision can usually be checked by the school (through the school nurse) or by your doctor or Health Centre. You may sometimes feel you are being a nuisance, but it is your child's education at stake, so be a nuisance.

A recognised way of tackling reading difficulties is by increasing the amount of 'structure' – that is, carefully planned and detailed support – in the learning situation. But what structure will work? Let's look at what should already have happened, by asking 'What help have you given your child so far?'

If your honest answer to this is 'very little' or 'none' then you ought to be reading the earlier chapters to take your first steps! If you feel that you have given a considerable amount of help, your next step is to analyse what you have done to see if a firmer structure is needed. Try putting yourself through some structure at this point, by asking yourself the following questions:

a: Have I read often *to* my child, books he/she really enjoys and is interested in?

b: Have we read together on a regular basis, at least three or four times a week?

c: Were the reading times convenient for both of us?

d: Do I really give my child adequate praise?

e: Do I get a little irritable when hearing reading? Do I show anxiety or impatience?

f: Is anything upsetting the sessions? e.g. Is the T.V. always on, are others continually interrupting?

g: Do I talk about the book with my child?

h: Is there anything about the sessions I am unhappy with?

i: is there anything about the sessions my child is unhappy with – have I asked whether there is?

j: Has my child's teacher suggested anything 'special' I need to do? Have I asked?

k: Are the books or materials we are using too difficult? Is my child happy to use them? Have I asked?

If you feel you have let anything slip, go back and attend to these basic principles first. There's no need to try other techniques unless you feel strongly that more or a different structure is needed. If you're sure about this, read on.

Many people think that the reason why some children do not learn to read is because they missed out on one or more stages in the reading process. Unfortunately few educators agree on what the stages actually are! Recently though, two people have managed to write down clearly a sequence of stages which have proved extremely useful in practice. Peter Young and Colin Tyre[5] suggest that if there were a really ideal way to learn to read, it might be as follows:

1. Lap reading. A child first learns through hearing rhymes and songs, and listening to a parent read in the security of the parent's lap.
2. Incidental reading. The discovery, with parents' help, of street signs, people's names, and the print on cereal packets and such like.
3. Shared reading. While listening to a parent read, the child follows the parent's finger across the page.
4. Reading as a pair. The parent first talks about the reading, then reads it aloud. Parent and child then read in unison. Then they read the same passage again, this time with the parent pausing occasionally to allow the child to supply some of the words. The child then reads the same passage alone, helped as necessary.
5. Prepared reading. The parent first talks about and reads the passage aloud with the child following ('shadowing'). The child then reads the passage silently, asking for any words that he or she does not know or understand. Then reads it aloud with help as necessary.

Young and Tyre produced some startling successes by getting parents to help their children through these stages, though many of the children had been labelled as having severe reading difficulties before. However do try to find someone who can help you (see chapter 11), as following stages like this can be quite a complex procedure. Young and Tyre expected parents to work with children for 30 minutes a day, every day for a year!

Another well thought-of technique is paired reading.[6] The trick of paired reading is to understand its two main elements, namely simultaneous and independent reading.

In simultaneous reading, you and your child read aloud together, ensuring that every word is said properly. The reading must not be so slow that the story is lost, or so fast that the child has difficulty in keeping up. This may sound easy, but you will find that practice is needed. In independent reading the adult stops reading, and the child continues alone. The change from simultaneous to independent reading is under the control of the child – you will have both decided beforehand what signal your child will give (e.g. a tap on the table or your leg, or a nudge). Whenever the signal is given, praise your child for the attempt at independent reading: this is most important. Methuen have published some books for children which explain this technique and have good stories (e.g. Awful Arabella, Spencer's Spaghetti, among others).

Paired reading is best used for relatively short periods of time, say 3–5 weeks, returning to the more general approach used in this book afterwards. And just because you are using paired reading does not mean that the other rules have changed! You still need to talk about the book, allow a choice of books, and keep the sessions regular and reasonably short.

Finally, there is one golden rule for parents of children with learning difficulties, and it can hardly be stressed enough: that is, try not to show your own anxiety. Indeed, as far as possible, try to avoid feeling anxious about a child who is taking time over learning. This may sound all very well for us to say – but your anxiety will help neither of you in the least, and may achieve the very opposite of what you want, by communicating itself to your child, and making him or her anxious in turn. And anxious children don't learn.

Whatever age or stage your child is at in reading, you should find the next chapter full of ideas for the kind of reading materials you can enjoy together.

Summary

Good readers: encourage your children to read widely; share your interests, and share theirs.

Reading difficulties: Check vision and hearing; analyse what has been done so far; try a different technique if necessary; always return to the overall approach of this book.

SIX

Ideas for Books and Reading Materials

You can never begin too early to develop children's reading and language skills. So in drawing up a list of possible books and materials, we have included some for the very youngest children, and we start with these. Don't forget that older children often enjoy books that were originally intended for younger ones. Books referred to in this chapter can be found in the book lists at the back.

Cloth, rag and board books. Most babies have a few of these given to them at one time or another, and they should be fairly inexpensive. They help very young children to see that pictures are used to represent real objects. When talking about the pictures use words your child understands – don't call a moo-cow a jersey heifer! These 'books' help children to enjoy language, and 'reading' them can become a favourite activity which is demanded time after time – as good as playing with them in the cot, or eating them.

Books from Christmas cards. A small collection of Christmas or birthday cards can be turned into a good, cheap book. Cut out the pictures until all the cards are about the same size, use a hole punch or the point of a sharp pair of scissors to make holes, and tie the cards together using string or ribbon – or a ring binder for real effect. Looking through these books gives endless pleasure – and older children enjoy making them for younger ones.

Nursery rhymes and nonsense rhymes. If any kind of book can easily be found it is a nursery rhyme collection. These rhymes have been enjoyed by generations, and tracing their history has been a fascinating study for adults. Besides being fun to recite and act out (e.g. Oranges and Lemons) they help children develop an awareness of rich and varied language at an early age. They are also easy to memorise, and form an important part of a child's pre-reading development. While your child enjoys them, keep reading them.

Children also thoroughly enjoy, and love repeating, simple nonsense verse. A good example of a book containing such verse is 'Inky Pinky Ponky'. There are many excellent books of nonsense verse produced now, and the sense of rhythm and enjoyment of words encouraged by 'Inky Pinky Ponky' can lead to the appreciation of other kinds of poetry.

Flap and pop-up books. Whoever invented these did a marvellous service to children's books. Very few of us have not enjoyed them at one time or another, and they are improving year by year. One flap book the very young enjoy is 'Where's Spot?' The puppy, Spot, is hidden and his mother tries to find him – there are flaps to lift up to see if he is there. Every child we have met has not only loved the story but has worn out the flaps from lifting them over and over again. At the risk of creating a shortage situation, we would suggest that this book must be on every child's bookshelf.

Pop-up books are becoming more and more complex and have reached exciting heights with books such as 'The Robot' by Jan Pienkowski. Few children, indeed few adults, can resist pulling and pushing the tabs which make some pictures move – though very young children may need an adult around, otherwise parts can get broken in their enthusiasm!

Because books like these tend to be expensive, you might hesitate before buying them – but we suggest that one book such as this, which stimulates so much, is worth ten cheaper books, and this may put the cost into perspective (see book list for further examples).

Photo albums and scrapbooks. Pictures of themselves and of people that they know ensure children's interest and spark off a lot of conversation and fun.

This can be taken further by helping your child to build up her or his own album. Besides photographs, it can contain simple words or short sentences, and a few mementoes (train tickets, newspaper cuttings, a pantomime programme etc.). Try a theme such as 'My Family', or 'Our Village' – this often goes down well with children.

Books without words. These tell a story using pictures only, and many schools give them to children before introducing reading books. Children enjoy them because they can tell their own imaginative story to the pictures. Many such books also appeal to adults, 'The Snowman' being one notable example.

Picture books. Every child should have some of these. Unfortunately they are usually expensive, but are read again and again and again. The true picture book relies both on words and pictures – take either away and the book loses its richness. Somehow the author must leave enough out of the text for the pictures to add to the story, but the pictures do not in themselves tell the story. Children love them, and if any kind of book is going to motivate them to read more it is a good picture book – initially read to them and later read by them, and probably read again in adulthood. There is such a wealth of good picture books that it is hard to single any out, but current examples include 'Rosie's Walk', 'Dinosaurs And All That Rubbish' and 'The Very Hungry Caterpillar' (see book list).

The print around us. Children can learn at a very early age that print is used to convey messages. Words are all around us, and can be pointed out to children long before you could expect them to read them. Street-signs, cereal packets, adverts, and all kinds of everyday items that children handle have print 'messages' on them. Children begin to associate printed words with chocolate bars and television programmes, and realise that the squiggles are related to the language they speak – this is a big step forward.

Your child's own writing. Use your child's writing as a source of reading material. We've talked about the importance of natural language, and understanding the meaning of the text – what could be more easily understood than what you have written yourself? This is in fact a very important part of learning to read, and should be encouraged wherever possible.

Making books with your child. This may sound like a difficult and time-consuming task which should be left to the professionals; but it really needn't be. Admittedly it is important that the end result should be as presentable as possible, so that you can both feel proud of your efforts, but this should not put you off. It is now possible to buy 'make your own pop-up books' (Bodley Head) which will give you a very professional finish, though the young child will need quite a bit of help to make them.

Much less elaborate but still successful books can be made very cheaply. Often children will enjoy making short books about themselves. Important family events can be written about or a holiday diary kept, perhaps using photographs. You can help in all kinds of ways: by providing brochures and magazines to cut up, by talking and asking questions, by giving workspace, but most of all by showing a real interest. Don't be too ambitious though – your child may never finish the book.

Write your own books. Have you thought about writing for your child yourself? The world changes year by year and it is easy to forget that our children do not have exactly the same childhood experiences as we did. A few hundred words about our own childhood could bring to life some of the conversations we have with our children. Why stop at this? Get on to Granny and Grandad, and other relatives who have led different or interesting lives.

Telling stories. The storyteller has almost disappeared in this technological age, and this is unfortunate. Up and down the country thousands of infants enjoy storytime every day, but usually from a book. Many of us think we do not tell a story well, and tend not to risk trying it with our children, but often we underestimate ourselves. Children love listening to made-up stories, and will forgive all sorts of hesitations and improbabilities. But if you really don't feel up to composing your own stories, then tell them true ones about yourself and your family – embellishing as need arises!

Taped stories. These can be bought over the counter at most newsagents. There are two kinds. In one the tape is just there to be listened to, in the other a book telling the same story comes with the tape so that it can be read as you listen. Both are helpful to children, and indeed teachers often use tapes in the classroom for a variety of reasons. One of these is to allow their pupils to enjoy stories, another is to encourage them to listen more carefully. But no teacher would let this activity be the only method used to develop listening or story appreciation skills. Although tapes are enjoyed by children, they can never replace real books or real conversation.

Humour. Everyone enjoys a good joke, and children are no exception. Anyone with a child of 7–11 years old can bear witness to the endless stream of terrible jokes which only children seem to love. There are now numerous books of jokes and riddles (see booklist) which can be read again and again, some of which can appeal to children as young as four and five years old. But this is not all. Many other books for children are written to make them laugh, and they will read them for this reason. Teachers and librarians will be able to keep you up to date with appropriate 'funny' books (see book list).

Books with social or emotional content. One of us tells the story of nine year-old Tim who was unable to read, and whose opinion of himself couldn't be lower. Then one day he was read 'Leo the Late Bloomer' (Puffin) which is about a little lion who was not able to do anything – read, write, draw, or eat tidily – but who 'blooms' in the end, finding one day he can do it all. This story had a dramatic effect on Tim, who read and re-read the book, and never looked back.

This story demonstrates the power of the printed word, and immediately suggests how books can be used to help children come to terms with their own feelings. If you believe your child needs help over some worry, it is usually possible to find a story which may be able to help. There are now books on the market which deal with virtually every difficult situation children can find themselves in, from the arrival of a new baby to divorce, from the handicapped boy next door to coping with mum going to hospital. But always remember that books will only help –

they cannot replace more personal ways of dealing with difficult problems.

We have included a few examples in the book list to demonstrate the kinds of titles that are available.

Specific interest books. As children get older, they will want to use books to learn more about topics in which they are interested. There is almost a glut of such books now, and you should be able to find appropriate ones for your child's interests. One of us has even managed to track down a book on snooker that was written at the right language level for an eight year-old to read. Consider buying those interest books that will be referred to often, and borrowing those that are likely to be read once and then shelved – children's passions can be very short-lived.

Newspapers, magazines and journals. Has your child realised how enjoyable these can be? A number of local papers now have special sections for children, many of which contain interesting activities for them to do. But why should children's interest stop at such specialist sections? Surely they are also likely to be interested in the local news, especially if someone they know is involved or an event they attended is reported? And why shouldn't they enjoy the cartoons in the nationals, or follow the fortunes of that illustrious club Manchester United – and don't most children quickly learn to check the evening television programmes? The reading potential in a newspaper is enormous, and few reading materials can be shared so easily.

All this applies also to magazines and journals, especially as your child gets older. Computer monthlies can be read and discussed together, and the knowledge gained applied immediately. 'Do-it-Yourself' and 'Good Housekeeping' can be jointly or independently read and the ideas discussed later. All this can enhance learning without additional expense – unless of course you don't take a newspaper or occasional magazine, in which case you will have already asked yourself the question, 'What reading do I do in front of my child?' (won't you?).

Reading for information. One of the crucial uses of reading is that it enables us to find information. Most of us read newspapers, 'hobby' magazines and, if we really have to, railway timetables. Why shouldn't we encourage children to do the same? From very early on we are used to our children asking the question 'why?' (in fact, can you ever forget that infuriating stage when every sentence appeared to begin with 'why?'), and this curiosity can be harnessed to develop their knowledge and reading even further. Instead of always giving them answers verbally, why not encourage them to seek the answers through the written word? So, unfamiliar words can be looked up in the dictionary, facts can be checked in an encyclopaedia, newspapers can be scanned to check the record of the local team, a visit can be made to the library to pursue personal interests; the possibilities are almost endless. Often young children will need guidance when learning how to use their reading skills in this way, and though they will be receiving a considerable amount of help from school, you can give them lots of extra practice. This allows them to follow the interests of the moment – something teachers are not always able to do easily in the busy classroom.

You will notice that we have not referred to graded 'reading books'. These are often cheap and obtained quite easily in corner shops, perhaps with the weekly shopping. These books may be useful, but can also be rather uninteresting. So when buying them, ensure that the pictures are interesting, that the language in the book is familiar to your children (that is, the language they use reasonably commonly in speech), and that there is a real story or useful information. Always bear in mind that you want to buy a book which will be read many times, not one which will sit on the shelf after one boring reading session.

Getting hold of books

The question now is: 'Where can I find good, stimulating books?'. The obvious answer is 'In a good bookshop', but there are other sources.

School. We hope that borrowing from your child's school is allowed, and indeed encouraged. School resources don't stretch far, but your child will probably be allowed to borrow books on most days. The more expensive books may not always be readily available for individual loan.

Local libraries. This is the single most important source of books for families. Libraries usually have a good children's section, and some are especially good at catering for the young child. Librarians can offer up-to-date information on which books the young enjoy reading – and this can save parents much hard searching and money.

School bookshops. Many schools run their own bookshops, and you can usually be assured that the books on sale have been vetted by teachers. Advice is readily given, and sometimes payment can be spread over several weeks. If your local school doesn't have such a bookshop, why not offer to help set one up?

School book clubs. Some firms now send booklists to schools, who distribute one to each child. These are popular as they provide a good, cheap source of books, and teachers should be able to advise on appropriate titles.

Your child may become very enthusiastic about the club and want to order books regularly. It is in this kind of situation that children's choices are liable to be strongly influenced by friends, or by publishers' exotic blurb, and this can lead to mild family strife! Try to handle an awful choice tactfully, and certainly don't feel that you have to buy club books.

Secondhand shops. These are always worth browsing through, and just occasionally children will find a real gem. Many markets have a secondhand bookstall.

Jumble sales. Jumble sales, school fairs and church fêtes always have an ample supply of very cheap books. The problem is that most of them are not in their first youth, and children should not be presented with very tatty materials. But a careful rummage may yield excellent bargains.

Library sales. Occasionally local libraries sell off books. It is unlikely that they will be selling popular or cherished books, but the shelf is always worth inspecting.

School 'swap shops'. These allow you to acquire new titles whilst getting rid of unwanted ones. Often they are held at special events such as school clothing sales. If they are not held at your local school, get a few of your parent friends together and organise one.

Family. Books as well as clothes can be handed around the family and passed down from older to younger children. You could also encourage relatives and friends to think of books for Christmas and birthday presents – but do give them some concrete suggestions.

**Caution*: While it is necessary to throw things out sometimes, don't dispose of any book your child may want to come back to, however tatty or recently unused. You should always ask your child first.

Footnote on free choice

Whether buying or borrowing books, from whatever source, parents may wish to exercise some control over their children's reading. This is a difficult problem, which has few solutions in the adult world. We do believe that parental views should be taken into account when choosing books, but if children want to read certain books they should generally be allowed to do so; then any 'controversial' issues can be talked through.

It would be impossible to summarise this chapter but we'd like to say:

Don't forget the libraries.

SEVEN

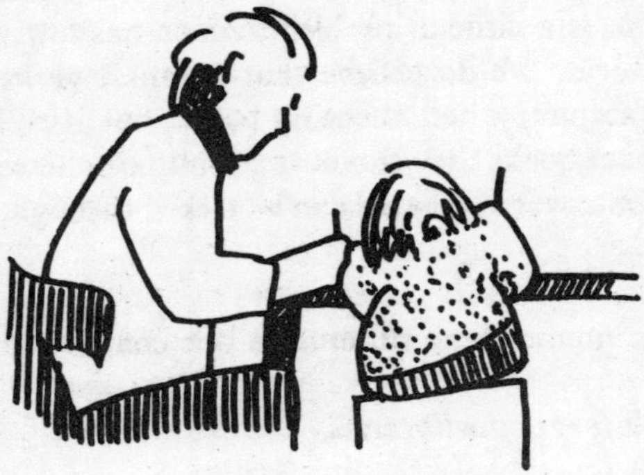

Learning to Write

In the last chapter, we included the idea of making books together, which will involve you in both reading and writing. The point we made at the beginning of this book – that different areas of learning cannot be separated from each other – is particularly true of reading and writing, which are closely linked, and will develop naturally together out of your child's experiences in daily life.

When we talk about 'writing', we are referring not to one skill, but a great many. Getting your ideas down on paper involves particular ways of thinking and understanding; it also involves the ability to make the necessary marks (handwriting) and to spell and punctuate. Although all these skills develop together, we thought it simpler to leave some of the 'technical' skills of writing – handwriting, spelling and punctuation – to the next chapter, and to concentrate first on children's creative writing: the way they express their thoughts on paper.

The beginnings of writing

You may well find that the early stages of writing come before reading in your child's life. When babies draw in the food they've spilt on the high-chair, they are making their first 'marks'. Next comes scribbling on paper – which probably gets more encouragement from you than the food idea – and from then on parents find themselves naturally admiring and asking questions about the meaning of the various shapes and scribbles that appear. Gradually the scribbles become more precise, and before long you are helping your child to form the letters of his or her name. Once children have grasped the essential point that squiggles on paper actually stand for something, then they are on the way to understanding writing.

If it is the child who has made the squiggle (or seen you do it), then the link between reading and writing is all the more firmly made, because of its particular personal meaning. Birthday cards are a good early way for children to make this sort of link – they enjoy writing names and messages for people they love. And when it comes to getting cards themselves, what could be more personal and important than the big figure 3 on the front of the card, and the message inside saying Granny sends her love, and has sent the big teddy bear for your special day?

Writing for a purpose

From the very beginning of scribbling on paper, you can make 'books' of your child's drawings. These will be like the other picture books you make together, except that in this case no one but the two of you is likely to be able to identify the helicopter or the concrete-mixer depicted on the page! That is where writing comes in. If the concrete-mixer is labelled, then Grandad too will be able to 'see' immediately what it is. When children realise what a difference it makes to adults to get the help of a bit of writing like this, they see that writing has a real purpose. Suddenly there's a whole new way of communicating with people.

A word of caution here. If each time your child makes a carefree squiggle, you immediately pounce on it and ask: 'What's that?' this can be a killer for spontaneity. No artist would stand for it! Giving names and labels to pictures, and making books from them, are just good ideas for things to do, among many others – not to be overdone. Sometimes you just admire, and leave it at that.

As your child gradually learns to write, through copying what you have written, imitating you when you write, and experimenting him or herself, there are many ways in which you can help the process along. If you are stuck for ideas, always ask yourself the question, as you did for reading:

WHY DO WE WRITE?

This question keeps adults on the right track when helping children, because it focuses on *purpose*. To begin with, children will write spontaneously because they enjoy it, and want to show off their skill, but soon they discover that writing has a purpose, and produces results. Your child sees you writing a note to the milkman, or making a shopping list, or writing a cheque, and can see *why* you are doing it. (The cheque, cashed at a bank, looks particularly rewarding, though children will find they don't get quite the same effect when they copy you on this one!)

You are in a good position to help your child understand why people write. Although teachers nowadays are very much aware of the importance of writing for a real purpose – the child's purpose, not the teacher's – we are not so far from the days when children wrote mostly to please the teacher. They simply wrote what was asked of them, because the teacher told them to, and not for a reason of their own. This is still bound to happen to some extent in schools. Nor do children often see teachers writing for their own purposes. You, on the other hand, are likely to provide this sort of model naturally, in the course of your everyday life.

Ideas for writing activities

Writing is an extension of talking – it's another way of telling each other about things. So try the following:

– write notes to each other, as a game: 'What do you want for supper?' – 'Fish fingers' (in the early stages, you provide the spellings, of course). Children enjoy answering this one with magnetic letters stuck on the fridge;

– pin up notices: 'Don't forget your football kit tomorrow; send messages in writing, instead of telling them direct;

– let your child try, much earlier than you might usually have thought of it, to print a few words on the typewriter or computer; different ways of doing things make learning exciting, and open up new ideas. We know of children who *started* to learn to write on the word-processor!

– get your child to tell a story, or give an account of something he or she did, or made, into the tape recorder. Then you write the story up. Children get a great boost from seeing a whole piece of writing that came from them, even though they wouldn't yet be able to write it for themselves. If you can type it, you'll probably be surprised yourself how good it looks. Once it's written, your child can read the story back to you, or to somebody else: reading your own writing, as we've said, is one of the best ways of learning to read.

– take other opportunities to write out 'in best' what your children tell you, or write themselves. By doing so you are saying, more effectively than you could in words, how much you value what they can do. When you turn out together a well-presented 'book', or something to go on the wall, you are making your child into an author – someone whose work is taken seriously by others. There is no praise better than this.

– find ways to share in your children's activities. Many of the above ideas will come naturally under the heading of 'play', which children are often (not always!) happy for adults to join in. All kinds of writing can come into children's imaginative play – think of doctors and nurses, shopping, and of course teachers! Encourage brothers and sisters to share writing activities. Just as children learn to talk, not by being 'taught', but because they want to communicate with other people, so they learn to write.

'Free expression' or accuracy?

Once children are learning to write for themselves, the awkward question of accuracy has to be considered. It's fine for you to neaten your child's work and turn out a good copy sometimes, but your eventual aim, of course, is to help the child do it for him or herself. There is a delicate balance to be struck between the 'free expression' of children's spontaneous writing, and the need to write correctly – or at any rate sufficiently correctly for other people to be able to pick up the meaning. There has been a long controversy in education between those teachers who place the main emphasis on 'free expression', which must not be thwarted, and those who insist on accuracy. The best path, as in so many things, lies somewhere in between.

However, there is no doubt about where the emphasis should lie in the early stages. Here, the adult's idea of accuracy hardly comes into the picture, and is not in the least important. The early stages of writing need to be allowed to develop naturally for themselves. Your very young child will not write in ways that you can recognise – it takes some time for sounds to be associated with written letters, and if your five year old writes 'fog jpt on mlb' and tells you it says 'The frog jumped on my lap', you should feel nothing but pleasure at how well things are developing.

Later, say by eight or nine years old, the picture is changing, and accuracy begins to matter more. Even now, you still need to be careful.

If you constantly point out where your child has gone wrong in spelling, punctuation and grammar, you will spoil the pleasure of writing for its own sake, and the child's pride in achievement. But if, on the other hand, you make no attempt to help your child to 'edit' work, you won't be doing any favours either. Accuracy does matter, because getting it right is what makes our work clear to others. It's a matter of consideration for the reader, and it's also a practical necessity if you want to be understood.

Nevertheless, of these two aspects we firmly believe that your first priority is to encourage children to write freely, so that their thoughts are not interrupted. Children write to have their say, sort out their thinking, and develop imaginative ideas – this is a process that has its own flow, and is best not disturbed. Ideas and imagination must come first. When you 'neaten' your child's work, don't change the actual words, or the structures of the language used. Remember you are trying to show that you value the child, and his or her language – if you do too much correcting, children feel the work is no longer their own, and lose interest.

Once children have had the chance to write freely, and had their writing enjoyed by others, then you can sometimes encourage them to go through their own work, editing it. Thus the first 'go' becomes a draft, which the child works on, just like an author. You can help by reading the work aloud and asking

a few questions: 'Is that what you wanted to say?' 'Is there anything you'd like to change?' At this stage you can point out spelling and punctuation mistakes, if your help is wanted.

Don't overdo your help. Writing correctly comes gradually, as children learn to read and criticise their own work like 'real authors'. Through their reading of books and other written materials, children gradually pick up the 'proper' way to order their words, to spell and punctuate. Too much well-meaning adult 'help' can actually get in the way of this process.

The final stage in turning out good work after editing is writing up a new neat copy. This stage can seem tedious, but you can make it worthwhile by the fuss you make of the work afterwards, showing it to other members of the family, pinning it on the wall, or sending it into school for the teacher to see. Remember here the importance of a real purpose – children need to know there will be readers of their work, and those readers have to matter to them.

Developing writing

Learning to write doesn't stop with being able to turn out a piece of original work, reasonably well presented. From now on you can encourage your child to explore different kinds of writing. There are a great many, ranging from keeping a diary, in a straightforward recording style, to the first efforts at creative poetry. Other kinds are: story-telling ('narrative style'); recipes and instructions; making lists and classifying (e.g. types of birds, and how one type differs from another); letters of all kinds; and so on. All these involve a variety of different styles of writing – we don't write a recipe as we would a poem, or a thank you letter like a technical brochure! As your child's reading ability expands, and as you share a wider variety of reading materials together, so you will discover different styles that you can experiment with.

Working with the school

We hope you will have been supported in all this by your child's school. Presumably you will see your child's school books sometimes, and these may give you ideas for the kinds of things to write about. We hope you'll also see the teacher and discuss ideas for your child in more detail.

Some schools ask parents, and grandparents, to write their own 'books', perhaps illustrated by their children. These are often about their own experience, or life in another country. The books are then 'published' by the school, and make wonderful reading material for the children: 'Jane's mum's written about Jamaica'; 'Philip's grandad worked in a circus!'. Or, parents and children can write books together: sharing their own language like this with the wider audience of school can bring the written word alive for children, and provide a lot of fun.

Some junior and secondary schools ask parents and children to write book reviews on books they have read together. This may involve filling in a simple form, in which you not only describe the content – the characters and plot, or the subjects covered if it's non-fiction – but also evaluate various aspects of the book. That is, you say what you thought of the way it was written, and whether it did what it set out to do. This sharpens critical judgement, and is very helpful to children in learning to discriminate the good from the bad.

Children who have learned to write evaluatively like this can be encouraged to join in the dialogue between teacher and parent on their own 'record card'. Even young children can do this on a simple level:

> 'Dad heard me read, he said I was coming on'
>
> 'The tiger book was very funny and very sad'
>
> 'I thought I chose a book about turbo-jets, but it was about gliders, so I was bored'

Older children can sometimes make quite sophisticated judgements about themselves:

> 'My reading has changed a lot. I used to choose books that were too difficult, I wanted to keep up with my friend. Then my Dad said I was being ridiculous. He found me an easy book on decorating, and we did my

> room together. After that I read the things I want to read, and now I understand better too' (10 year-old girl).

If you and the teachers have helped your child to express thoughts, feelings and judgements like this in writing, it will be an achievement to feel proud of.

Finally, please remember: however much or little contact you have with the school, home is an excellent place to discover the purposes of writing. Don't curb your imagination, or your child's, when it comes to putting things down on paper.

Summary

1. Let reading and writing develop naturally together – in jobs around the house, in play, etc.
2. Make 'books' out of your child's first drawings, and later write out their writing 'in best' for them.
3. Talk to your child about what you yourself are writing, and why – so that he or she can see that there are real purposes in writing.
4. Use the tape recorder, the typewriter, the computer.
5. Freely expressed 'creative' writing is a priority over 'editing' – accuracy matters, but comes gradually through reading.
6. Help your child explore different kinds of writing for different purposes.
7. Talk to the teacher about your child's individual writing style, and problems. Join in any projects the school may have – don't be shy about your own skill as an author!
8. Remember – home is a very good place to learn to write, and to enjoy writing.

EIGHT

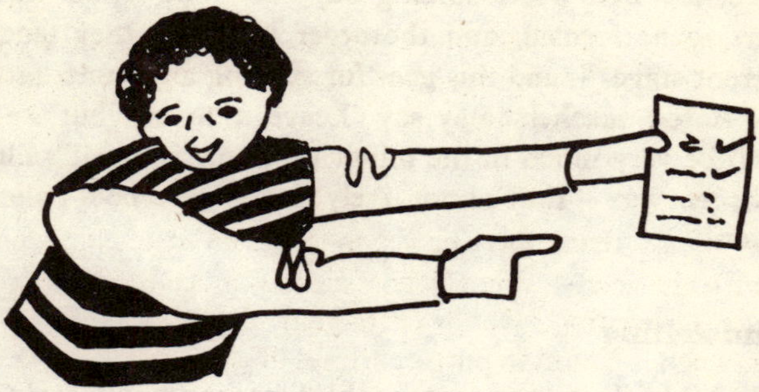

Handwriting, Spelling and Punctuation

This chapter deals with the more 'technical' aspects of writing – with getting writing right. We have talked about the importance of making writing presentable, and readable by others: here are some ideas on how you can help your child to do this. Don't be discouraged if it takes a long time to 'get writing right' – this sort of accuracy does not come easily. For that matter, it sometimes does not come at all: some brilliant people never learn to spell, and the inability of doctors to write so that anyone else can understand their scrawl is legendary. Writing is a difficult skill – or rather, a whole series of different skills that have to be put together – and you will need a lot of patience. Through it all, keep it in mind that your child's original ideas are the first priority, and accuracy comes second.

The presentation of writing can be roughly divided into three areas: handwriting, spelling and punctuation. For each of these, we'll give some basic ideas which are unlikely to clash with what your child is being taught in school. Even so, schools may have strong ideas of their own. In handwriting, for instance, it's well worth finding out how your school likes the letters to be formed, and the order in which they teach the different stages – and this goes for spelling and punctuation as well. A few teachers may say 'Leave it to us', but we hope they'll be very much in the minority. Show yourself willing to do it *their* way – they're not likely to change school policy just for you!

Handwriting

Your child will start to practise this literary activity early in life – quite possibly on the wallpaper. Your aim, having persuaded your child to write on more suitable paper, is to help get the squiggles into the right shapes, laying the foundation for future handwriting.

The basic shapes. Letters can be grouped into 'families', according to their shapes and the way they are made:

1. The 'o' family starts at the top and goes round in an anticlockwise direction (*Fig. 1*). The other letters in this family follow the shape of the letter c, which starts from a little further round the top than the o; e starts in the middle, but follows the basic shape after that.
2. An easy family is that made with the simple downstroke and loop (*Fig. 2*).
3. Then there's the upside-down version of the loop (*Fig. 3*). This family is trickier, because of the way the initial down stroke has to be partly retraced.
4. Just two letters (*Fig. 4*) are left over without a family.

Not everyone makes their letters exactly like the ones opposite, of course. Sometimes, for instance, b is made as it is in print. This would put it in the family of 'n' – as a 'tucked-in h'. Then again, there's a whole collection of letters that can just be made up of straight lines: k, x, z, w, and so on. The trouble with these is that they don't easily convert into 'joined-up'

Fig. 1

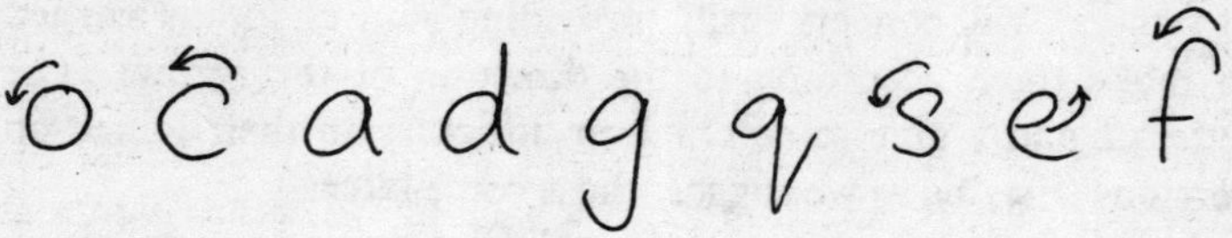

Fig. 2

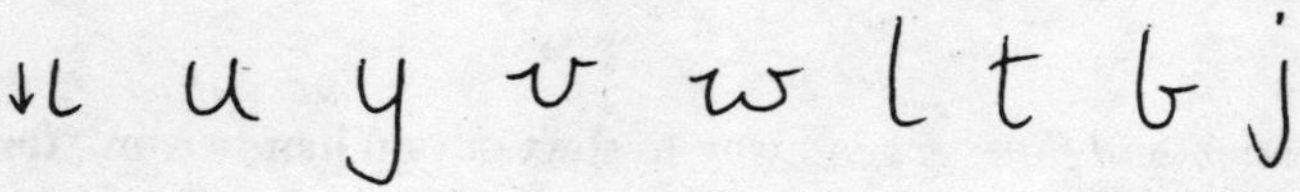

Fig. 3

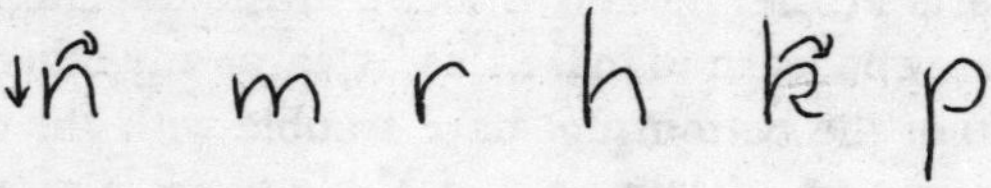

Fig. 4

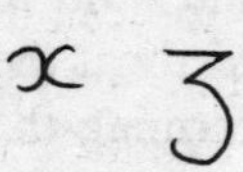

Fig. 5

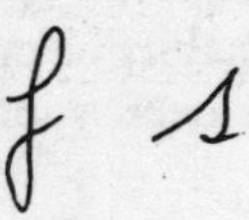

Fig. 6

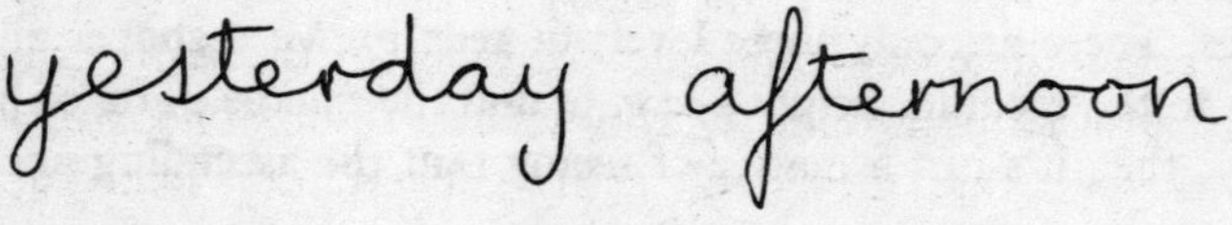

writing later. All the versions we have given (with the exception of f and s), will convert easily, providing your child has learned to make them according to the direction of the arrows. The letters f and s give some children difficulty in their joined-up versions (*Fig. 5*), so we suggest those come later.

Most of the letters we use in ordinary writing are in lower-case, as in the illustrations, and these are the ones to teach first – capital letters can come later, linked to the rules of punctuation.

Direction and flow. A good way to start out on handwriting for most children is to get the letter 'o' right. It's the basis of many other letters, and is a nice simple circular movement that comes naturally to children quite early on. The trick is to make sure your child's 'o' starts at the top and is made in the direction illustrated. Children who learn to make this letter, or any other for that matter, from the bottom up, have trouble with their handwriting later, because it's almost impossible to get a nice easy flow of joined-up writing if you start your letters 'on the line'. This is a good reason to give your child plain paper to write on at first. If children try to work from lines, they're inclined to use the line as a kind of safety-position, and want to start all their letters from it, instead of starting correctly at the top of the letter. Not only does this mean they're forming the letters wrong, it also gets them worried about trying to write 'straight' when there's no need for this in the early stages. Much more important is to get a good flow in the movement of the letters, and to make them in the right direction from the start, so that the muscles of the hand get into 'good habits'. Try the good old method of letting your child write over your writing, to get the idea.

Later you can introduce lined paper, and explain the differences between the tall letters and those that go below the line. Letters of even height look far better than straggly, uneven shapes. There are only three levels to keep to. Most shapes all come to the medium height – e.g. o, and the middle parts of h and y; then it's just a matter of seeing that the ascending and descending parts of letters all come to the same height or depth: e.g. h, l and g, y.

Cursive script. Children are ready at different ages to start linking the letters up into cursive script (the technical term for 'joined-up writing'). Some children find it easy to go from one letter to the next without stopping, others seem to find it difficult. There is no need to put pressure on – during their teens they will sooner or later decide to write the adult way, and all the more easily if no particular fuss has been made. Incidentally, if you have an older child who has failed to learn to write properly in the first place, don't concentrate on trying to improve the individual letters separately – just go straight into joined-up writing. This has the double advantage of saving face by not going back to 'baby' printing, and even sometimes being easier to pick up when you're older, because the shape of the links help to form the following letter.

If your child has formed the letters as we have shown, or in a similar way (there should be nothing rigid about handwriting, everyone's style is different and the important thing is to teach for clarity, rather than a particular style), then it should not be too difficult to link the letters together. But not all that simple, either – an eight year-old can find it quite a struggle to master the art of making the links between letters smoothly. Links vary according to the letters they connect – look at the number of different links in 'yesterday afternoon' (*Fig. 6*). Don't feel you have to link all the letters, especially in long words – there are sometimes natural pauses where a link can be left out, and if most of the letters are linked, the word will still look 'joined-up'.

We don't have to insist on special rules for making links – more important is to get a relaxed flow, encouraging gentle loops and swings rather than sharp, straight lines and corners. Two helpful ideas we have found to encourage this process are those of the roller-coaster, swinging from point to point, rolling, curving and diving – and the jet aeroplane doing stunts, sometimes 'crashing' where it goes straight down to the line, as in the letter n. These ideas can make for a rather noisy lesson, but increase the fun.

Spelling

The irregularity of English spelling is notorious. There are in fact complex rules which govern our spelling, but for most of us these are too complicated to remember, and not necessary anyway. We are not concerned here with the rules, but with a method that helps children to spell correctly.

First though, we need to remind ourselves that most children will learn to spell most words quite naturally, through their reading and by having help with correcting their own work. These are activities that have a meaning for the child. As with all your child's learning, keep the idea of purpose well in mind – adults can too easily forget this in areas like spelling. It is interesting that many six and seven year-olds can spell 'police' and 'ambulance' easily, as they are important words with special meaning, whereas they will mis-spell (just as they mis-read), apparently simple words such as 'on', 'no', 'they', 'what'.

Children need to learn to spell words that are familiar to them: there is little point in knowing how to spell words they never or rarely use. Spelling should never be taught in isolation, but should be based on children's own written work. If that written work has been done for a purpose, and if your child knows it will be read and appreciated by someone he or she cares about, then there will be a real reason to spell correctly. (Mind you, Granny may *like* funny spellings, so don't let's get too serious about it!)

One obvious skill you can encourage is the use of a simple dictionary: there are some excellent children's dictionaries available, some of them attractively illustrated. Then, if a word keeps cropping up as a mis-spelling, show your child the following procedure.[7] It's called 'Look, cover, write and check':

1. Write the word on a blank page.
2. Look carefully at the word.
3. Cover up the word, and then try to write it.

4. Compare your effort with the original.
5. If it's right, go to (6) below.
   If it's wrong, go back to (2) above.
6. Try to write the word successfully three times in a row (even five times for awkward words, or very bad spellers).
7. Check the spelling a day or two later.

Don't rush this procedure, and explain it carefully – if a child doesn't use it methodically it won't be so successful.

If teachers send home lists of spellings, these can be learned in the same way. Make sure your children know the meaning of the words on the list and how to use them. For example, get them to give you a sentence using the word before writing anything – and if they can't, give them some examples. Remember spelling is as much associated with meaning and understanding as are reading and writing.

Punctuation

Punctuation, like handwriting and spelling, is about making your writing understandable by others. To a great extent, correct punctuating depends on a child getting the 'feel' of a sentence – where it begins, where it ends, and how it is supposed to sound to the reader. How can you help with this? It's not difficult to explain that sentences begin with capital letters and end with full-stops, but it's not so easy to explain to a child just what a sentence actually is.

What is a sentence?. We may say it's a set of words that make complete sense in themselves, but children hear 'sense' in all kinds of things. They may pepper their work with full-stops after each little phrase – or more likely, forget about full-stops altogether, and still feel their writing makes sense. Nor is it likely to be more helpful to go into the formal structure of a sentence, with its noun and verb. Whether or not you believe in teaching formal 'grammar', it is not neat arrangements of grammar we are after in helping children to write, but the ability to express ideas on paper, and to communicate those ideas to others. Grammatical terms may come in useful later, but not, we believe, for basic punctuation, which is based more than anything else on commonsense. It's based on the rhythm and 'feel' of language too, and writers need some flexibility in the way they punctuate.

To take an example, let's suppose your child writes: 'The major and the corporal, side by side, looking fierce.' We know there's something missing here, but how will you explain that to your child? Not wanting simply to demand a 'verb', you might ask: 'What were they doing side by side? – you haven't told us'. This sort of question often works very well, but it isn't foolproof. In this particular case you're asking for the perfectly logical answer: 'Looking fierce'! The fact is that the child who wrote this 'sentence' isn't so far from getting the idea. If your eight or nine year-old can put capitals and full-stops in likely places, so that the main ideas are separated from each other by full-stops, not too far apart, then probably you can rely on your reading together to take care of further progress naturally.

Learning from reading. It's from talking, listening and reading that children pick up the 'shape' of a sentence. Language goes in rhythms – speak and pause, speak and pause – and the best way to help your child to pick up sentence patterns is by reading aloud, and getting the child to read to you. You can point to the full-stops sometimes, to show how they carry out the job your voice does. It's particularly useful to read your child's work aloud to each other. Where there are no full-stops, or too many, the results can be hilarious. But make sure this really is a joke, and doesn't become hurtful criticism – remember your child is the author of what's been written, and authors do feel sensitive about their efforts!

Beyond the full-stop. Once your child has mastered the idea of a sentence, the rest of punctuation is not so hard to grasp. It may not get used much in the heat of the creative moment, but a session of cool editing afterwards will sort that out. What is the child editor checking for? Once the basic sentences have been checked for capital letters and full-stops, your child needs a checklist:

a: More capitals. Any names? Days of the week?

b: Commas. Do some sentences need a bit of a rest in the middle? Are there any lists, needing commas between the items?

c: Speech marks (inverted commas). Does anyone say anything? (Check again: does what they say start with a capital letter?)

d: Question marks. Does anyone, including the writer, ask anything?

e: Exclamation marks. Does anyone shout? Make a joke?

f: Apostrophes. These are tricky. Either they show where a letter or two has been missed out (you've, it's, etc.), or they show that something belongs to someone (the captain's jacket, the buttons' shiny surfaces).

Many adults don't get their apostrophes right, or put in ones that shouldn't be there – you've only to look at the greengrocer's window showing bean's, apple's and banana's! So don't expect your child to get this one right in a hurry.

Then there are the more sophisticated forms of punctuation: the semi-colon (a bigger rest than a comma, not such a complete break as a full-stop); the colon (the first part of the sentence is pointing you to the next); the dash; and the bracket. None of these is likely to be fully mastered before secondary age. Even more than the previous list, which to a great extent 'goes by the rules', these more advanced marks need to be understood from reading the work of published writers.

And that's the note on which to end our chapters on writing. Good writing is learned most of all not by being corrected, but by 'taking in' the work of others. That's yet another good reason to make sure your child gets the opportunity to read widely, among books of good quality. We go on learning to write all our lives – and that includes published authors, who are always striving to write better.

Summary

1. Don't get anxious about accuracy – it comes gradually.
2. Check on the school's ways of doing things.
3. Handwriting: don't impose strict rules of style. Teach some basic 'good habits', but mostly go for the 'flow'.
4. Spelling: make sure your child can use the dictionary; for tricky words, use the 'Look, cover, write and check' technique.
5. Punctuation: try to help your child get the 'feel' of a sentence – rules may not help much. Point out sometimes how writers in the books you are reading together have made their ideas clear to the reader.
6. Purpose comes first. If children are writing for a reason they can appreciate, and if they know who they're writing *for*, then it's worth their getting writing right.

NINE

Helping with Mathematics

It is easy to help children with mathematics, as it surrounds our every move. Bus numbers, bills, times of day, maps, cooking, woodwork and so on all need some small knowledge of mathematics. Unfortunately though, it is surely the subject that most scares people. Many of us feel our mathematical foundations are weak (probably due to bad teaching rather than inability). If you believe you have a 'mental block' with mathematics do read on – we believe you will find it a lot easier than you think.

The essence of helping your children is to use all the mathematics around them in such a way that they will enjoy learning about it. Nowadays teachers try to give children lots of practical experience, problems that need solving and opportunities to practise what has been learned – all of which you can also do. Of course, as your children get older you may approach the subject a little more formally (when helping with homework for example), but in the earlier stages everything can be treated as fun.

These early stages of mathematics don't depend on the ability to read, but they do depend on language. Through simple mathematical language, very young children can be introduced to all kinds of concepts. The ideas and activities which follow are aimed at giving children plenty of opportunities to explore mathematics. We don't expect you to do them all – even teachers find it hard to cover all the topics – but we hope they will help you come up with ideas of your own, so just explore those activities your child will enjoy. We would also like to stress that the following suggestions are not in any special order, and many of them can be used at different ages.

A final word to the unsure. Many schools run workshops to explain how mathematics is taught nowadays: you will be greatly encouraged by going to these. If the school doesn't do this, ask for it to be done. Meanwhile, talking with the teacher will probably give you much of the information you need.

Sorting. Children will need to be able to sort things into different groups and categories, and this is one of the features of 'set theory' as it is currently taught in most schools. Sorting bricks according to their colour or size is an obvious example. Others include:

- Buttons by shape, colour or size
- Cutlery into different drawers (and why)
- Kitchen equipment into 'for cooking' and 'for eating with'
- Toy animals by name (pigs, cows etc.); or as 'pets' and 'not pets'
- Clothes – as worn by boys or girls, washed/not washed, every-day/best
- Transport models, as public or private
- Crayons, pens, felt tips by colour
- Plastic letters by 'has curved lines' or not.

Indeed virtually anything can be sorted in some way, even to the extent where you are sorting things by their constituents (wood, glass, plastic, iron and so on). We do have one reservation about sorting activities, and that is that children are sometimes expected to do too much of them. Children can sort from quite an early age, and tend to play at sorting quite naturally, so why labour the point? You are often in a strong position here compared with teachers, as you are more likely to know whether your child can cope with any particular sorting task.

Comparing. Children need to learn the language of comparison. Words like 'bigger, smaller, more than, less than, equal to' can be brought into all kinds of practical situations. In the kitchen, one egg may be 'bigger' than another, you may need an 'equal' amount of flour and sugar (try using 'same' and 'equal' together to aid understanding); in the garden you may need to sow 'more' cabbages and 'fewer' cauliflowers.

Shapes are particularly good for comparison – try using bits from games (the ones that contain wooden or plastic shapes); compare circles and squares, big and little triangles – talk about them and why they are different.

Matching. Matching of like with like is a special form of sorting. There are numerous chances to allow the practice of this skill:

- Snap, the ever-popular card game. Many other card games also include matching ('Old Maid', 'Rummy').
- Lego: when playing with this you can match shape and colour, and later according to the number of connectors. Many construction toys lend themselves to matching in this way.
- Dice – two or three used together.
- Lotto – an ideal game.
- Teatime: is there a knife matched to each place? Has each person got a sticky bun?
- Dominoes.

Most games you play with your child will give you the opportunity to practice matching.

Counting. Being able to count is of fundamental importance, yet many children do not master it at an early enough age. We need to learn the actual words, to use these to count actual objects, and later to count in our heads. So every child needs plenty of practice at it.

When children are young, count everything: the cups, the cars, the knives, people, books, toys – even count the number of clothes the child is wearing. And don't forget occasionally counting out loud as a game to see how far the child can get, especially for the very young child. This is something that teachers cannot always devote enough time to.

Numbers are also needed to order things, and it is important for young children to learn about this. So encourage them to say and use 'first, second, third' etc.

Estimation. In this world of computers and calculators it is crucial that we do not lose the capacity to estimate. Machinery can give us accurate answers, but if either we or the machine make a mistake, estimation will stop us making total fools of ourselves! So children need to develop their ability to guess in all kinds of situations: do I take a five or ten pound note to buy today's shopping? How many tins might be needed to feed seven? How long should it take to drive to Borchester? How tall can I expect to be next year? and so on. As children get older they will become more and more sophisticated in the art of estimation – allow them plenty of practice, and encourage it in all mathematical activities, including games.

Sets. Most children today come across the concept of sets very early in their school life. Unfortunately, many adults claim they can't understand it themselves – but by sorting and matching and doing things with everyday objects they have actually taught children the elements of set theory! A set is simply a 'collection of things', and 'set theory' is about what you can do with sets (e.g. a set of knives can be added to a set of forks to form a set of place settings). Once you know this you should be able to understand what your children are talking about, and learn from them. If they can't explain the more difficult aspects to you, then perhaps the teacher has not explained adequately to them – put this to the teacher, and ask for help for both of you. Once you have grasped what is involved you will find lots of applications, and it is these everyday applications that makes the study of sets so important to the young.

The lesson here, as with any unfamiliar maths topic, is to know what your child is doing at school. We feel you are entitled to know, so you can help in the practice of the new skill, and also so that you won't expect too much of your child. For example, just because decimals are being taught doesn't mean that your child can solve the problem 'petrol is 41p a litre, how much would 2.57 litres cost?'!

Quantity. Activities to help develop quantity concepts are found in many daily jobs – all you need do is involve your child in these. Any job requiring measuring or weighing, or the concepts of volume and area, can be used.

– Cooking. At first children can help by counting the number of sausages or whatever. Later they can do some of the weighing (we recommend checking afterwards!). Later still they can follow simple recipes.

- Mixing cement. This starts to introduce the idea of ratio and volume – though you need not use these words at first.
- Home decorating. Think of all the measuring that this requires. Painting, carpeting, and wallpapering can also bring in the measurement of area.
- Shopping. This provides countless possibilities. Talk about buying milk in pints and petrol in litres, compare containers and how much they hold.

Regular shapes. The important shapes are the square, circle, and triangle. Other more exotic ones include the pentagon – famous for its military implications, and the hexagon – the shape bees prefer. Irregular shapes mustn't be forgotten: count the number of sides and try to describe them.

You can draw them or paint them, you can cut them out of card or wood or cloth and use them to make pictures and patterns, you can find them in everyday articles (e.g. saucers are circles). Indeed you can see and work with shapes almost anywhere. What is important is that your child can eventually recognise a shape and give it a name.

Look together at the three-dimensional shapes, like cylinders, pyramids and cubes. Don't forget other words which are also used in understanding shape: corners (vertices), edges, bottoms (bases), faces (the sides of a pyramid, for example) and angles. Many toys are constructed in ways that are useful for showing what these words mean.

Symmetry and asymmetry. These are important concepts. Draw and cut out first a square and then a donkey. Fold these down the middle to see which has two matching halves, and which is asymmetrical.

Co-ordinates and graphs. That old game 'battleships' is good for teaching the elements of graphs and co-ordinates. The important point is to get your child to give the co-ordinate across the page first, followed by the one up the side. This then corresponds with the X and Y axes as mathematicians use them. If 'battleships' does not appeal for some reason, the game can easily be adapted. For example you can both hide treasure in your grid, and then by guessing the grid reference try to pinpoint where the other has hidden it.

Learning to map-read is an ideal way to help children understand co-ordinates, and can be linked to family walks and car rides.

Look for opportunities to make graphs. Marking the height of children on a wall in the garage can form a graph, if done with several children, or over a period of time.

Fractions. We cut things in half and divide cakes into eight portions without always realising that we are dealing with fractions. It is sharing these tasks that will give children the language and understanding of fractions. Perhaps you could spend a little more time on some activities: for example, if you have cut a cake into 8 pieces which are the same, you could demonstrate the fact that if you put two together you have a quarter, and so on.

Plasticine or pastry dough cut up can lead to simple fraction understanding, including addition and subtraction. As your child gets older you can use similar techniques: share (divide) plants in half before sowing, share a block of ice-cream into

seven equal portions, divide the time before lunch into thirds to make sure everything gets done, and so on.

Decimals. Like fractions, this topic seems to be a bugbear for many people. Tackle it entirely through the handling of money – something we can all understand!

The four rules (+, –, ×, ÷). These have been left until last, as they feature in every aspect of mathematics. This does not mean they have to be taught boringly. Too many children spend too much time doing thousands of little sums. Of course practice is important, as without it simple arithmetic wouldn't become second nature. What is really required though is an understanding of the rules. So instead of sitting your child down to work through sums (though this may be helpful sometimes) use opportunities that arise every day. Simple problems are constantly cropping up which you can ask your child to help you solve – after all it is for such problems that most mathematics is needed. How many cups are needed if two people are leaving? How many logs are we burning each day? What will the change from the chemist be? and so on. If your child finds division difficult, remember our tip for decimals: they may not know 48 divided by 3, but if 48 pence has to be shared with two sisters you can bet on few errors being made!

Calculators and computers. Few educators believe that children should be denied access to these. They are valuable aids, especially in mathematics. Try to ensure your child has some experience of them.

Mathematical opportunities

Shopping. Shopping, day-trips and pocket money provide ideal opportunities for teaching about money and its value. Spending it, saving it, losing it are all important. Involve children in financial exchanges, introduce concepts such as change-giving, banking and 'interest'.

Games and play. Join in your children's games. The 'pretend' play of the young will give numerous opportunities to use mathematical concepts – pretend shops and post-offices are good examples. Encourage sand and water play, and don't forget all the traditional games (indoor and outdoor) which you probably play from time to time anyway.

D.I.Y. Helping with this will encourage all kinds of concepts, and gives you a chance to use words such as angles, edges, areas, centimetres (we're sure you no longer work in inches!) and cost. If children are to learn though they must **do** something. Let them actually do the measuring or whatever – you can always check afterwards.

Homework. When this is set, it helps you to find out what is being done at school, and to learn about the topic. Start early with your children's homework, it helps you to keep up with them!

Novelty. There are lots of things on the market these days which can help extend the understanding of mathematics. Three-dimensional models can be made from card; wood or card mosaics can be used to form patterns; we've even seen a crib that can be made from polyhedra (solid shapes).

Walks. Even a walk can give you a chance to talk maths. Point out the symmetry of leaves and of reflections in the pond, use the compass directions, compare the shape of a pillar-box with a cylinder, and so on.

Travelling. A car journey can give you many opportunities to encourage the use of mathematics:

Distances: how far have you travelled? How far to go?

Speed: as children get older they can work out averages, and even the estimated time of arrival; in the early stages fast and slow speeds can be compared.

Maps: encourage your child to follow the map route in

the car, it gives ideas of distances and develops a sense of direction.
Counting cars, lorries, caravans not only passes the time but gives practice to young children.
Road signs can be compared for shape and meaning.

Tailpiece

We have continually stressed the importance of fun – don't make maths a bore for children by overdoing it. We hope you now feel able to tackle some mathematics with your children, even if you started this chapter sceptically!

Summary

1. Don't worry about your own mathematical ability – you can do it!
2. Help your child to develop the language of mathematics.
3. Be practical: use mathematics to solve problems that arise daily – most activities have a mathematical component.

TEN

Learning at Secondary Age

As children gradually become adults in their own right they often seem to get more expensive, more demanding and more difficult. When talking to other adults, whether difficult or not, we don't treat them as children, and when working with secondary age children we need to strike the balance between working with them as adults and as children – never an easy task.

Many of the ideas we have discussed for primary age children can still be extremely useful in the early years of secondary school, and your child will quickly let you know if any are wrong or inappropriate. The areas you can help with most are: continuing to develop language, helping with homework, and acting as a good model yourself. We'll look at each of these in turn.

Talking and language

We have stressed the importance of language throughout this book, and its continuing development should always be a priority. Conversation especially continues to be important. Discussing world news, local football matches, and family predicaments all develop a facility with language: the motto is 'don't just do things together, talk about them'. In the same way you can continue to support the development of reading and writing in the ways we have already discussed.

Homework

Homework, or indeed any other activities connected with school, can also be talked about – at noisy length in some households! It is the predicament of every parent, no matter how well educated themselves, that homework is fraught with problems, usually to do with the subject matter. Somehow it was different in our day, or the subject causing most difficulty is the one we are not too good at, or we just don't understand the textbook or the teacher's instructions. The real skill when helping to tackle your child's homework is not in knowing the answer, but in knowing how to find out the answer. The other important skill is being able to persuade your child to get the work done in the first place!

One way forward is to help children with the actual management of their learning. By this we mean helping them to organise their workload, and develop strategies to cope when faced with difficulties. The skills needed to do this are often called 'learning skills' because they enable children to learn more effectively.

It is really beyond the scope of this book to cover this subject in any great detail, and you will find further reading in the book list. But here are some ideas to start you off.

1: Persuade your son or daughter to make a list of homework, plus any other activities he or she wants to do during the coming week. Then both look at the list and plan the activities for each evening, revising the list at the end of each week in the light of experience. Ensure an adequate amount of time is spent on disliked subjects as well as those enjoyed. The older the child, the less she or he will be prepared to accept your proposals, though gentle guidance may be acceptable – in other words, negotiate rather than dictate.

2: Encourage children to think about the time when they work best, how often they need a break, whether they prefer to work in silence or not (some really do work better with the radio on), and persuade them to use all this information when planning how to work.

3: When helping with homework try to establish exactly what has to be done, and then plan a way forward. This may be unwelcome to children at first because it can be rather time-consuming, but do persist as they are likely to accept it and do it themselves when they find it saves time in the end. For example, if they have been set homework in history they need to establish:

- do I need to write an essay or a few paragraphs?
- what has to be included (i.e. what is the teacher looking for)?
- how much do I need to look up, and how much do I already know?
- where do I find information I haven't got?
- what do I need to do first?
- in what order should I carry out the steps?

This at first sight may sound pedantic and cumbersome, but can save hours of wasted time and effort. Incidentally, if more children questioned themselves as carefully as this in public exams they would have far greater success. So many children fail just because they don't read the exam question properly, and answer exactly what it asks.

4: Establish the habit of using reference books, text books and libraries when working with your child. It is unlikely that you will always know the answer, and anyway it is obviously important to teach children 'how to find out'.

5: Encourage your child to use different reading skills. Children are often taught about these at school, and it may be worth talking to your child's teachers. Four common styles are skimming, scanning, receptive and intensive reading. When skimming the idea is to look at such things as the title, the contents page, the headings, and the illustrations, with a quick glance through the text, to get a general impression of the book. This helps to decide whether a book is useful for what is wanted. Once you have the right book, then scanning can be used. Here the eye quickly scans through the text to find relevant information. Both these techniques are regularly used without thinking by adults – e.g. looking through the Radio Times.

A book such as a novel is usually read just to absorb its meaning (receptive reading); whereas sometimes parts of a book will need to be read very carefully, with some re-reading of sections and even note-taking, so that the reader can achieve a thorough understanding of its contents (intensive reading). If you encourage these techniques, and you probably do without always realising it, your child can pick them up from you and practice them, as well as being taught them in school.

6: Exams create different problems, and revision is the bugbear of every youngster, but if habits such as those listed above become second-nature then revision will be slightly more bearable.

The model parent!

All the above will help, but it is your example which will have the most effect. Are you seen reading sometimes? Do you talk about things you have read? Have you got some historical or geographical interests, if only when on holiday? Do you take an interest in the world of science and technology? Do you belong to the local library? Try to engage yourself actively in your

child's learning. Consider the following:
- pass the newspaper around noting an interesting story
- mention books that you have read and enjoyed
- read books your child has read, then you can both talk about them afterwards
- use a dictionary and reference books when you yourself want answers (perhaps you could start by finding out the characteristics of an axolotl?)
- always explain long or difficult words, look up precise meanings if necessary
- give the occasional book as a present, not one you feel they ought to read but one they would like!
- involve your youngsters with forms; even tax forms are interesting, including your rude comments about tax inspectors!
- try to share your son's or daughter's interests without making them feel you are being too 'nosey'
- share your own interests (the football pools, knitting patterns, the greenhouse, breeding armadillos), though don't force interests on them
- when working on the car or cooking, use manuals and recipes: this shows the value you place on the written word, and may also improve your cooking and your car.

By and large, adolescent children will welcome your help and interest in their learning, but guard against intrusiveness. Your child is growing up and needs to become gradually independent of you. Be sensitive, and watch out for hints.

School contact

As secondary schools are large and complex institutions, with children coming into contact with many more teachers than in primary schools, it is usually much more difficult for parents to work closely with teachers. This can be frustrating for all concerned, though some schools are finding ways of overcoming the problems. For example, many schools have newsletters which keep parents informed about virtually every aspect of school life, while others have homework files with special guidance given to parents as to how to help with homework. Secondary schools sometimes hold meetings for parents on various aspects of the curriculum, and a few have held workshops for parents on topics such as mathematics.

Such initiatives by teachers do not always meet with a good response from parents, perhaps because they feel they are expected to take an interest rather than invited to be involved, or because there is just not enough personal contact with the teacher to keep the parent interested. Whatever the reason, if parents really supported such ventures it would be much easier to encourage the school to take further and more acceptable action. Teachers do get demoralised if parents don't respond to ideas, and because time, energy and money are precious, do not persist. Therefore the message for you is: support meetings, contribute to newsletters, encourage any of the school's ideas to make further contact with parents.

Of course, some secondary schools have developed schemes similar to those found in primary schools, which means there are proper channels for you to contribute to learning. Teachers have usually worked hard to set them up, and the organisation of them can be quite complex. If you feel they're not quite right, make your opinions known – but be patient, as changing them can be a delicate and expensive business in a large school with many departments.

If a school has no schemes for working with parents, you can still talk to teachers and school governors (don't forget the parent-governors), get other parents interested, and discuss issues on open days.

In this day and age such discussions often bring about change, even if it is only small. Keep trying and good luck.

Summary

1. Help with the organisation and management of work.
2. Act as a good model yourself – be perfect!

3. Strike a balance between helpfulness and intrusion.
4. Take every opportunity to co-operate with the school.

Above all, talking with your secondary age children saves many more problems than it creates – get into the habit.

ELEVEN

But It's Not Quite So Easy for Us . . .

If you follow the advice in this book and work with the school wherever possible, you will probably overcome most of the difficulties in your way. Some may remain though, and we will try to tackle those that parents have commonly brought to our attention. The question that comes up most often is:

But where can I find the time?

Time is a commodity none of us has – yet somehow it has to be made, and while this is not easy, it can be done if there is the will. Regular reading times pose the greatest difficulty, in that ideally a time should be found on most days. Try analysing your day: can you find a regular time first thing in the morning, or immediately after tea, or just before bedtime? Can you share such activities with another adult – could grandparents or neighbours help? If time is a serious problem, try to be realistic in your aims, and just read with your children as often as you can.

We're afraid we cannot agree with anyone who says they haven't enough time. Only a few minutes at a time are required, and children need it – especially yours.

I've got five children . . .

Having more than one child often means they can look after one another, though you will be needed to sort out the fights and arguments that seem to happen on more than the odd occasion. The real problem is ensuring that each child receives some individual attention, whilst bearing in mind that the others need to be occupied in some way. Consider one or more of the following:

- In a two-parent family tasks must be shared. Perhaps one can help an individual while the other supervises activities – even if it is only watching television.
- Can older children in the family help younger ones? This is not always satisfactory, and should not be allowed to replace you entirely, but does allow for many more individual sessions.
- Can grandparents, favourite relatives, neighbours or friends help?
- Be realistic as to how often you give individual attention. For example, a bit of reading three times each week is better than six days in a row, then nothing for weeks.
- Make good use of the weekends when time is more flexible.
- Look carefully at your day. The larger the family the greater the need for organisation, otherwise chaos ensues. So can your day be organised differently, perhaps freeing time in the evening?
- Try having sessions with more than one child at a time. This

would create no problems when you are reading to them, and when the children are doing the reading they can take turns.

- It is possible to show a high level of interest while doing other things. Listen to the children and talk to them – encouraging this in the family will stimulate the whole of family life.
- If one of your children is having a difficulty with learning, then this may be your priority. Try not to ignore the others, and give them some indication as to why you are giving one member special consideration.
- Ask the school if there is anything in particular you could concentrate on, or if they have any ideas on how to give maximum benefit to a child, given the circumstances. The school may be able to give your child a little extra help if the situation warrants it.
- Numerous opportunities arise during the day to help your children to learn. When you're not too busy, keep an eye out for them.

The big family, though more wearing for parents, can be an asset to children, who learn from their brothers and sisters. Use its assets to the best advantage, and accept that you may not always be able to give as much individual time as single-child families – remember they haven't got your advantages.

I'm not too good at the 3R's myself

Not long ago a researcher found that if children with reading difficulties spent a short time simply talking with an adult each week, their reading improved.[8] This should give confidence to those who believe their own ability is limited. It really does not matter – what matters is that you find ways to support and encourage your child.

If you hear your child read you will quickly pick up the mistakes, even if your own reading is poor. If you hear 'The cat sat on the vivisectionist' you can be pretty sure it is wrong. Neither does your inability stop you from talking about books –

tackle the issue with confidence. The younger your child, the easier you will find it, and the more you will learn together. We have known parents who actually learned to read from reading easy books with their children. We don't know who gained most from the experience, the parent or the proud child who 'taught' Mum to read. Similarly with other subjects – by talking with your child, you will find ways of helping them. The object of the exercise is not to do things for children, but to work with them.

Don't feel shy about admitting your own difficulties to the school. How can they advise you without knowing that you have a difficulty? They won't tell anyone without your permission, that would be a breach of professional confidence. Teachers want to help your child, and a knowledge of your problems may explain things about your child they could not understand.

I just can't get my child to settle down . . .

Some parents, though very close to their children, find it difficult to settle down with them for a few minutes without a battle. If this is the case after trying the ideas in this book, don't feel your child need suffer. You just need to find other strategies!

Your first strategy is to drop everything for a few weeks, hoping that you are both just going through a bad patch. It may then be possible to build up gradually, starting with a few minutes only, always stopping before any sign of a battle.

If this doesn't work, ask yourself if someone else can help – your wife or husband, an uncle or neighbour. We know of one child who continually came to blows with his mother, whereas he was quite happy to learn with his grandad. Later his mother was able to take over when her son found that working with an adult was quite fun.

Discuss your difficulties with the teacher of course – he or she may be able to give ideas to deal with your particular child. Continue to work together in areas where your child is prepared to accept help, or try areas you haven't tried before. Children can be perverse – don't battle, just bide your time; sooner or later you will be asked for help.

All this time, your child needn't have lost out by not settling down to work. One of the best of all learning experiences is, luckily, one that most children will accept – and that is having a good book read to them at bedtime. And of course you will have been using learning opportunities while shopping, cooking and travelling – won't you?

Seeking help outside the school

It should always be the teacher from whom you first seek advice or assistance, and in our experience teachers have usually been very helpful. Just occasionally though, parents wish to seek the help and advice of other professionals. If you are doing this because you think a teacher is being obstructive or unhelpful, first ask yourself the following questions:

- have I actually talked with the teacher?
- have I given the teacher all the information needed?
- is it that the teacher has actually been quite helpful, but I haven't acted on the advice?

– have I been given advice I don't like, though it may be right?
– have I unfairly criticised the teacher?
– have I tried talking to the headteacher?
– have I asked for further advice?

If you are satisfied with your answers, you can seek further help from your Local Education Authority (L.E.A.), whose address and telephone number you can get from the school or the local library. These have professionals specifically employed to work with schools, teachers and parents, as well as children. For example, they have teachers to advise schools on how individual children or groups of children can be helped. Usually such people have been good teachers for many years before taking up their advisory posts. Their job titles vary across the country, but education offices and most schools will tell you who is available locally.

Such advisers, inspectors and special teachers are not the only people who can help. Every L.E.A. has educational psychologists to work with children and their parents. Like advisers, they can be contacted through the school or the local education office, and sometimes through doctors. The word 'psychologist' makes some people apprehensive – but educational psychologists are fully qualified teachers and know a lot about how children learn, so don't avoid them just because of the name. If you're at all worried, ask to meet one.

If you believe your problem is similar to one that others in the country are concerned about, there may be a national or local group who can advise you (e.g. The Children's Legal Centre can advise on certain legal matters). It is not easy to be specific here, but if the school cannot help you to contact such groups, advisers and educational psychologists usually can. Alternatively, ask at the Citizens Advice Bureau or at the local library.

These are, perhaps, the best ways to seek help outside the school, but some parents prefer to seek private advice, and are prepared to pay for this. Before buying such advice, try to find out what you will be getting, and check the qualifications of the consultants concerned (the L.E.A. will help here). We know a number of parents, for example, who have paid teachers to teach children to read, but who have not employed specialists. Often they have wasted their money. You don't pay an electrician to do the work of a plumber, so why employ the wrong specialist teacher?

If you really feel you are not getting anywhere within the L.E.A., try writing directly to the Education Officer, or contact your local Councillor. Such action may get things moving, provided that after hearing your case the Officer or Councillor believes that you have been unfairly treated.

If you believe your child has special educational needs, you can invoke the 1981 Education Act. If the L.E.A. agrees that your child has such needs, it must meet them under this Act. The Act is a very powerful tool for parents, but it is complex – though organisations such as the Advisory Centre for Education (A.C.E.) can help you. This centre advises on many aspects of education and publishes pamphlets and booklets, including some which explain how the Act works.

Whatever your problem, don't give up. With a little thought and help from others, virtually any difficulty can be overcome.

Summary

1. Time: examine your day carefully.
2. Large family: look for its assets.
3. Poor reader yourself? You can still help.
4. Your child won't settle? Don't worry, use the opportunities you have.
5. Seeking help out of school: try to talk to the school first.
6. There are many sources of help: don't struggle on alone.

TWELVE

Conclusion

In this chapter we'll try to give an overview, and point to new areas. In particular, what about all the school subjects we haven't covered in the book? We have concentrated on the basic skills that underlie the curriculum, but we hope we've made it clear that all kinds of other learning will be going on at the same time.

We must repeat that learning can't in 'real life' be carved up into neat bundles in the way our chapter headings suggest. The world of education concentrates on particular aspects of learning, for convenience – and when you sit down to help your child with difficult spellings, you're not likely to be thinking of the mathematical possibilities in the situation.

But if you're playing Peter Pan and Captain Hook with a six year-old, it's a different matter. You might draw the skull and crossbones on black material and make a flag; draw a map and mark the place names and where the treasure is hidden; calculate distances and count the fighting forces on each side; talk about real pirates, what they did and why; and so on. In this game, there lie the possibilities for 'lessons' in the school subjects of biology, needlework, art, spelling and handwriting, geography, maths, drama, history – and probably more that we haven't spotted! For your child, this game is *not* a collection of subjects – it's a game. But the learning, with the help of an adult who's on the lookout for the possibilities, takes place nonetheless – and probably more effectively than if you'd taught in a more formal way.

The same applies when you're helping an older child to follow an interest. Suppose you make a survey of the different kinds of birds in your area, find out their habits and write up a diary of the birds observed: we could be talking about classification of species, urban and rural environments, conservation, how to write up observations accurately, sketching, even making graphs to record density of bird population, and so on. It may sound rather grand put like this, but if you think about it, you will perhaps be surprised at how much you are already doing, just by pointing things out to your children and answering their questions in daily talk. By going into matters a little deeper, you can pull out further possibilities for learning.

Besides this informal approach through play and interests, there are other ways of taking part in your child's learning across the whole school curriculum. Perhaps the most obvious is through books. As children grow older, the books they read, whether from school or elsewhere, tend to be of the kind that give more and more information. Sooner or later, you will find yourselves touching on science and technology, history, geography and other school subjects – just through reading interesting books that are out to teach children something.

Teachers may arrange this with you in a more deliberate way. For instance, if the class is learning about windmills, the teacher may send home a book or an information sheet, perhaps with questions, for you and your child to read, talk about and work on. This is a great help to the teacher – and to your child, who comes to the work prepared. Similarly, work started in school can be 'followed up' at home. Learning about a particular topic like this gives a focus to what you're doing together, and has the added advantage of linking you very closely to what your child is doing in school. So one way and another, your home reading can lead you into many areas of the school curriculum.

If you can make the time, keep a few notes on your child's learning. Teachers keep records because it helps them to see where they're going, where they've got to and where they want to go next. From this they can plan clearly to benefit the children. Keeping your own records can help you in the same way, and will also enable you to communicate more usefully with teachers. Records are pleasant to look back on, for both you and your child – they give you a shared sense of achievement, telling you how far you've come together.

Once again, you are probably wondering where the time and energy is coming from to tackle all this learning. You may feel we have already covered a great deal of ground in the earlier chapters – and now we're talking about the whole curriculum! Surely a parent isn't expected to do the teacher's job, as well as all the work parents traditionally have to do? Added to which, many parents now both work full-time, and many are raising children on their own without a partner. It looks as though we're asking for that super-parent.

Well, the answer is that of course we're not. We are well aware of the strains most parents are under, and we don't want to add to them. What we would like to say is this:

- By playing with your child sometimes, and keeping your eye open for learning opportunities
- talking with your child in the course of your everyday life, and listening to what he or she says in return
- sitting down together for short reading sessions on most evenings, or sometimes other sorts of work as we've suggested

You will find that these things can actually take off some of the stress. You will be doing something constructive toward your child's learning, and that's something most of us worry about at some time or another. More than this, you'll find it fun, and as often as not relaxing – you get to know your children better, and you take from them as well as they from you. The message is: drop 'grown-up' work for a bit, and enjoy yourselves.

The one thing we *can't* say is that you don't matter where your child's learning is concerned. If you decide that sitting down to more 'formal' kinds of help is not for you, then do it all the other way:

TALK and PLAY

Nothing could be more important for children's development, and their successful learning, than these two crucially valuable activities. How lucky for us that they are enjoyable too.

BOOK LISTS

References

1. Bullock Report (1975) *A Language For Life*. Report of the Committee of Inquiry appointed by the Secretary of State for Education and Science. (London, HMSO)

2. Tizard, J., Schofield, W. N. and Hewison, J. (1982) *Collaboration between teachers and parents in assisting children's reading*, British Journal of Educational Psychology, 52(1), 1-15.

3. Griffiths, A. and Hamilton, D. (1984) *Parent, Teacher, Child*. (Methuen, London)

4. Widlake, P. and Macleod, F. (1984) *Raising Standards*. (Community Education Development Centre. Coventry)

5. Young, P. and Tyre, C. (1983) *Dyslexia or Illiteracy*. (Open University Press)

6. Topping, K and Wolfendale, S. (1985) *Parental Involvement in Children's Reading*. (Croom Helm)

7. Peters, M. (1985) *Spelling: Caught or Taught – A New Look*. (Routledge and Kegan Paul)

8. Lawrence, D. (1973) *Improved Reading Through Counselling*. (Ward Lock Educational, London)

Books Referred to in Chapter 6

1. *Inky Pinky Ponky* by Mike Rosen and Susanna Steele (Armada)
2. *Where's Spot?* by Eric Hill. (Heinemann & Puffin)
3. *The Snowman* by Raymond Briggs. (Hamish Hamilton & Puffin)
4. *Rosie's Walk* by Pat Hutchins. (Bodley Head & Puffin)
5. *Dinosaurs and all that Rubbish* by Michael Foreman (Puffin)
6. *The Very Hungry Caterpillar* by Eric Carle. (Hamish Hamilton & Puffin)

7. *Robot* by Jan Pienkowski (Heinemann)

Some Pop-Up Books

See You Later, Alligator by Tony Bradman (Methuen)
How Many Bugs In A Box? by David A. Carter (Orchard)
This Little Pig by Colin Hawkins (Macmillan)
Winnie-The-Pooh A Pop-Up Book by A. A. Milne (Methuen)
Haunted House by Jan Pienkowski (Heinemann)
Little Monsters by Jan Pienkowski (Orchard)

Popular Picture Books

Burglar Bill by Janet & Allan Ahlberg (Heinemann & Mammoth)
Each Peach Pear Plum by Janet & Allan Ahlberg (Puffin)
The Lighthouse Keeper's Lunch by Ronda & David Armitage (Deutsch & Puffin)
Mr Magnolia by Quentin Blake (Cape & Armada)
Willy The Wimp by Anthony Browne (Julia MacRae)
The Story Of Babar (Series) by Jean de Brunhoff (Methuen)
Would You Rather . . . by John Burningham (Cape)
Dear Zoo by Rod Campbell (Campbell Blackie & Puffin)
The Trouble With Mum by Babette Cole (Armada)
But Martin by June Counsel (Corgi)
The Enormous Crocodile by Roald Dahl (Cape & Puffin)
War And Peas by Michael Foreman (Puffin)
It's Your Turn, Roger by Susanna Gretz (Bodley Head)
Alfie Gets In First by Shirley Hughes (Bodley Head & Red Fox)
Titch by Pat Hutchins (Bodley Head & Puffin)
Mog The Forgetful Cat by Judith Kerr (Collins & Armada)
The Tiger Who Came To Tea by Judith Kerr (Collins & Armada)
The Quangle Wangle's Hat by Edward Lear, pictures by Helen Oxenbury (Heinemann & Puffin)
Not Now, Bernard by David McKee (Andersen & Sparrow)

Five Minutes Peace by Jill Murphy (Macmillan)
We're Going On A Bear Hunt by Michael Rosen, pictures by Helen Oxenbury (Walker)
Where The Wild Things Are by Maurice Sendak (Bodley Head & Puffin)
Can't You Sleep, Little Bear? by Martin Waddell, pictures by Barbara Firth (Walker)
Dr Xargle's Book Of Earthlets by Jeanne Willis, pictures by Tony Ross (Andersen)
Stanley Bagshaw And The Mad Magic Mix-Up by Bob Wilson (Hamish Hamilton)

Humorous Books

Flat Stanley by Jeff Brown (Methuen)
The Eighteenth Emergency by Betsy Byars (Bodley Head & Puffin)
Ramona The Pest by Beverley Cleary (Hamish Hamilton & Puffin)
The BFG by Roald Dahl (Cape & Puffin)
My Naughty Little Sister by Dorothy Edwards (Methuen & Mammoth)
Bill's New Frock by Anne Fine (Methuen & Mammoth)
Spencer Spaghetti by Bill Gillham (Methuen)
The Shrinking Of Treehorn by Florence Parry Heide (Viking & Puffin)
Tintin (Series) by Hergé (Methuen & Mammoth)
The Turbulent Term Of Tyke Tiler by Gene Kemp (Faber & Puffin)
George Speaks by Dick King-Smith (Viking Kestrel & Puffin)
The Great Smile Robbery by Roger McGough (Viking Kestrel & Puffin)
The Paper Bag Princess by Robert Munsch (Annick & Hippo)
The Worst Witch by Jill Murphy (Puffin)
Jacob Two-Two Meets The Hooded Fang by Mordecai Richler (Puffin)

How To Eat Fried Worms by Thomas Rockwell (Piper)
Clever Polly And The Stupid Wolf by Catherine Storr (Puffin)
The Elephant And The Bad Baby by Elfrida Vipont & Raymond Briggs (Puffin)
Harry The Dirty Dog by Gene Zion (Bodley Head & Puffin)

Examples Of Books With Social Or Emotional Content

Topsy And Tim Meet The Dentist by Jean & Gareth Adamson (Blackie)
I Can't Hear Like You by Althea (Dinosaur)
Miffy In Hospital by Dick Bruna (Methuen)
I Am Adopted by Susan Lapsley (Bodley Head)

Poetry Books

When We Were Very Young by A A Milne (Magnet)
Now We Are Six A A Milne (Magnet)
Please Mrs Butler by Allan Ahlberg (Viking Kestrel & Puffin)
Tiny Tim chosen by Jill Bennett (Armada)
Figgie Hobbin by Charles Causley (Macmillan & Puffin)
Twiddling Your Thumbs by Wendy Cope (Faber)
Revolting Rhymes by Roald Dahl (Cape & Puffin)
Sky In The Pie by Roger McGough (Viking Kestrel & Puffin)
Song Of The City by Gareth Oswen (Collins & Armada)
Gargling With Jelly by Brian Paten (Viking Kestrel & Puffin)
The Hypnotiser by Michael Rosen (Deutsch & Lions)

A Few Joke And Riddle Books

The Ha Ha Bonk Book by Janet & Allan Ahlberg (Puffin)
Spooky Riddles by Marc Brown (Collins)
Giggles Gags And Groaners by Joseph Rosenbloom (Sterling)
The Funny Side Of School by Roy Shipperbottom & Carolyn Webster (Nutmeg)
The End compiled by Richard Stanley (Puffin)

Books About Reading

Help Your Child With Reading by Wendy Body (BBC)
Reading Begins At Home by Dorothy Butler & Marie Clay (Heinemann)
Learning To Read by Margaret Meek (Bodley Head)

Books For Mathematics

The Parent And Child Programme: Parents' Guide To Your Child's Maths by Ruth Merttens. (Parent And Child)
Mathskill 1 by Peter Smith (and other titles). (Piccolo)
Multiplying and Dividing by Annabel Thomas (and other titles, plus workbooks). (Usborne)

Books About Books

Will You Read Me A Story? by Tony Bradman (Thorsons)
Babies Need Books by Dorothy Butler (Penguin)
Children's Books Of The Year (published regularly) by Julia Eccleshare (Andersen)
Treasure Islands by Julia Eccleshare (BBC)

A Selected List of Cedar Books